Tolle . . . lege . . .

— Augustine, *The Confessions* III/32

Take and Read

SPIRITUAL READING:
An Annotated List

EUGENE H. PETERSON

WILLIAM B. EERDMANS PUBLISHING COMPANY
GRAND RAPIDS, MICHIGAN / CAMBRIDGE U.K.

REGENT COLLEGE PUBLISHING
VANCOUVER, BRITISH COLUMBIA

First published 1996 by Wm. B. Eerdmans Publishing Co.

255 Jefferson Ave. S.E., Grand Rapids, Michigan 49503 /

P.O. Box 163, Cambridge CB3 9PU U.K.

Published jointly 2000 with

Regent College Publishing

an imprint of Regent College Bookstore

5800 University Boulevard, Vancouver, B.C. V6T 2E4

Published in association with the literary agency of

Alive Communications, Inc.

1465 Kelly Johnson Blvd., Suite 320, Colorado Springs, CO 80920

Printed in the United States of America

04 03 02 01 00   8 7 6 5 4 3

Library of Congress Cataloging-in-Publication Data

Peterson, Eugene H., 1932-

Take and read: spiritual reading: an annotated list /

Eugene H. Peterson.

p.   cm.

Includes index.

ISBN 0-8028-4096-5 (paper: alk. paper)

1. Spiritual life — Christianity — Indexes.

2. Spiritual life — Christianity — Abstracts.   I. Title.

BV4501.2.P428   1995

016.248 — dc20   95-44351

CIP

Regent College Publishing ISBN 1-57383-166-2

For
Steven F. Trotter
who knows how to read a book

Contents

Take and Read

Introduction

Spiritual reading, designated *lectio divina* by our ancestors, has fallen on bad times. It has always been a prized arrow in the quiver of those determined to cultivate a God-aware life, but has suffered a severe blunting in our century. This particular arrow has lost its point more through ignorance than indifference or malice, ignorance of the sense that "spiritual" carries. For the modifier "spiritual" in spiritual reading does not refer to the content of what is read but to the *way* in which a book is read. Spiritual reading does not mean reading on spiritual or religious subjects, but reading any book that comes to hand in a spiritual way, which is to say, listening to the Spirit, alert to intimations of God.

Reading today is largely a consumer activity — people devour books, magazines, pamphlets, and newspapers for information that will fuel their ambition or careers or competence. The faster the better, the more the better. It is either analytical, figuring things out; or it is frivolous, killing time. Spiritual reading is mostly a lover's activity — a dalliance with words, reading as much between the lines as in the lines themselves. It is leisurely, as ready to reread an old book as to open a new one. It is playful, anticipating the pleasures of friendship. It is prayerful, convinced that all honest words can involve us in some way, if we read with our hearts as well as our heads, in an eternal conversation that got its start in the Word that "became flesh." Spiritual reading is at home with Homer as well as Hosea.

Spiritual reading, for most of us, requires either the recovery or acquisition of skills not in current repute: leisurely, repetitive, reflective reading. In this we are not reading primarily for information, but for companionship. Baron Friedrich von Hügel once said it was like sucking on a lozenge in contrast to gulping a meal. It is a way of reading that shapes the heart at the same time that it informs the intellect, sucking out the marrow-nourishment from the bone-words.

*　　*　　*

For Christians the Bible is the primary book for spiritual reading. In the course of reading Scripture, it is only natural that we fall into conversation with friends who are also reading it. These leisurely, relaxed, ruminating conversations continue across continents and centuries and languages by means of books — and these books offer themselves for spiritual reading. After a few years of this, as with the Scriptures themselves, most of our spiritual reading turns out to be rereading. C. S. Lewis once defined an unliterary person as "one who reads books once only."

But leisurely and repetitively doesn't mean slovenly or lazily. G. K. Chesterton said there was a great difference between the lively person wanting to read a book and the tired person wanting a book to read. Nicolas Berdyaev represents the lively spirit: "I never remain passive in the process of reading: while I read I am engaged in a constant creative activity, which leads me to remember not so much the actual matter of the book as the thoughts evoked in my mind by it, directly or indirectly" (*Dream and Reality* [Macmillan, 1951], p. 13).

The necessity for alert and ready responsiveness to the Spirit is on display in a diary entry by Julian Green for October 6, 1941: "The story of the manna gathered and set aside by the Hebrews is deeply significant. It so happened that the manna rotted when it was kept. And perhaps that means that all spiritual reading which is not consumed — by prayer and by works — ends by causing a sort of rotting inside us. You die with a head full of fine sayings and a perfectly empty heart."

Walt Whitman gives the same counsel from a different angle: "Books are to be called for, and supplied, on the assumption that the process of reading is not a half sleep, but, in highest sense, an exercise, a gymnast's struggle; that the reader is to do something for himself, must be on the alert, must himself or herself construct indeed the poem, argument, history, metaphysical essay — the text furnishing the hints, the clue, the start or framework. Not the book needs so much to be the complete thing, but the reader of the book does" (*The Portable Whitman,* ed. Mark Van Doren [Viking Press, 1945], p. 468).

*   *   *

I have a friend who became a Christian as a young adult, and then was ripped off and exploited by unscrupulous, predatory religious leaders. Disillusioned, he wandered off into the world of alcohol and drugs and spent the next twenty years trying to get his spirituality from chemicals. One day in the mountains of Mexico, on a hunt for drugs, he met some drug dealers who had recently become Christians. They talked to him about Jesus, prayed for him, and he reentered the Christian way. Back home in Canada, he knew he needed support in his new life, but because of his earlier experience with religious leaders, he was wary. One day he went into a bookstore and asked the manager, "Do you have any books by dead Christians? I don't trust anybody living." He was given a book by A. W. Tozer, and for the next year read nothing but Tozer — a "dead Christian." From there he cautiously worked himself back into the company of living Christians, in which he is now a most exuberant participant.

Most, but not all, of the books in my list are by "dead Christians." That means that they have been tested by more than one generation and been given passing marks. That means that what these Christians have written has been validated by something deeper than fashion or fad. But my list does not pretend to be balanced or inclusive or authoritative in any way. It is personal. Many important books are not included, some out of ignorance but many others simply because they have not yet become important to me personally.

Mark Van Doren once wrote in a poem, "Omission is murder." I hope this is not always true, for I have omitted some of my very best friends. The absence of Asian, African, and Latin works of Christian spirituality is conspicuous — and the most regrettable of my omissions. I have come on them late in my life. I considered inserting what seem to me to be the best and most representative of them, but decided that since they had not yet become a part of *my* spirituality, it would not be honest. But I am reading them most avidly. Perhaps, if there is a later edition of this reading list, I can repair this deficiency.

Some of my annotations are only a few lines, others a page or more. The reader should not attach signficance to either the variations in length nor the order in which they are listed. I *browse* through my books. A passing glance can be as revealing as a lingering pause. The annotations are moments of attention I choose to share with my friends.

Lists like this have a way of expanding unconscionably, so I have imposed a limit on myself: twenty categories of not less than ten and not more than sixteen books in each category. Many of them transcend their categories — spiritual reading tends to do that. Not all of them are explicitly Christian — some I would classify as para-Christian, nudging in alongside the Christian faith but not explicitly declaring or embracing it. What they all have in common is that they have been used by our Lord the Spirit to deepen and nourish my life in Christ, sometimes in ways they almost certainly did not intend.

*   *   *

Not all of these books will become *your* books. Can I suggest a goal? Goal-setting is, for the most part, bad spirituality. But there can be exceptions. I think this might qualify as an exception: over the next five years, develop your own list of spiritual friends. Start with my list, but then gradually remake it into your own. You have to start somewhere. Start here. Eliminate. Substitute. Develop your own list, which over the years will become not a "list" at all, but a room full of friends with whom you have "sweet converse."

Luther, recommending one of his favorite books, wrote, "Indeed, this book does not float on top, like foam on water, it has rather been fetched out of the rock bottom of Jordan by a true Israelite" (quoted in *The Theologia Germanica of Martin Luther*, trans. Bengt Hoffman [Paulist Press, 1980], p. 42). It is a recommendation I like very much and pass it along attached to each of my book friends.

Unfortunately, many of the books listed here are no longer in print, but that's what libraries and used bookstores are for.

I

Basics

This list is necessarily arbitrary — it consists of *my* basics, not yours. But I strongly feel that every Christian needs such a list. It is protection against dilettantism: dabbling is a besetting sin in spirituality. These are the books I feel that I cannot do without. They have proved to be formative for me in two dimensions, personal and vocational, and have been a primary means for integrating my personal life of prayer with my vocational life as pastor and teacher. In trying to recover integrity in my vocation, and to stay mentally and spiritually alive as a Christian in this specifically twentieth-century North American environment, these writers are my mentors.

1. Charles Williams, **THE DESCENT OF THE DOVE** (1939). When I started reading Williams, I was a sectarian, "related" only to a small coterie of people who lived and thought and prayed like me. When I finished, I was part of a congregation centuries deep and continents wide. I started with a spirituality that was almost totally subjective; then I found myself in something large

— creational and incarnational. I'm not sure this is what Williams intended, but it is what happened. "Unintended consequences" are common in spirituality.

2. Hans Urs von Balthasar, **PRAYER** (1961). This is simply the best book on prayer that I have ever read. It is also difficult. Difficult because it is profound, theologically comprehensive, and spiritually rigorous. Balthasar, a Swiss Roman Catholic who died a few years ago, was one of the most capacious minds of the century. But he was, in addition, one of the rare people who seemed to have practiced in his heart everything he thought in his mind and wrote with his pen. This book is not only about prayer, but gives the unmistakable sense that the author is, in fact, praying.

3. Baron Friedrich von Hügel, **SELECTED LETTERS** (1927). A layman, von Hügel was a spiritual director of great wisdom in England in the early decades of this century. He lived on a private income and gave a lifetime of attention to the life of the Spirit and to the spiritual lives of his contemporaries. There is a kind of Germanic ponderousness in the way he writes, but I find him to be the most sane, balanced, and wise mind/spirit of my acquaintance. By sinking himself into the deeply lived truth of the centuries, he provided a mature center for many others in his counsel and writings. He was absolutely impervious to the fads and fashions in both culture and church that swirled around him like flies.

4. George Herbert, **THE COUNTRY PARSON** (1632) and **THE TEMPLE** (1633). Herbert lived in England in the sixteenth century. His *Country Parson* is a manual of pastoral theology; *The Temple* is a sequence of poems on the life of the Spirit in the context of being a parish priest. Together, they serve as a kind of "outside" and "inside" combination for vocational spirituality.

This is one of the rare opportunities we have of seeing a first-class pastor at work in both dimensions, inner and outer.

5. Augustine, **THE CONFESSIONS** (A.D. 397–401). Spirituality involves taking our personal experience seriously as raw material for redemption and holiness, examining the material of our daily lives with as much rigor as we do Scripture and doctrine. *The Confessions* is the landmark work in this exercise.

6. Gregory the Great, **PASTORAL CARE**, translated by Henry Davis (1950). A pastor reflecting prayerfully and wisely on pastoral work. Given the very nature of pastoral work — to be immersed in the particulars of one congregation and culture — it is amazing how similar the work continues to be from sixth-century Rome to twentieth-century North America.

7. Gregory of Nyssa, **THE LIFE OF MOSES**, translated by A. Malherbe and E. Ferguson (1978). Gregory's glory is his devout imagination: he reads Scripture wildly, extravagantly, curiously. But he is all the time disciplined to a pilgrim faith, subjecting his playful imagination to sober obedience.

8. Karl Barth, **THE EPISTLE TO THE ROMANS** (1933). Barth wrote this commentary while pastor of a small congregation in the Swiss village of Safenwil. I read it when I was pastor of a small congregation in Maryland. I was trying to learn how to be a pastor in a territory bordered on one side by a believing (or semi-believing) congregation, on the other side by an indifferent (and occasionally scornful) world, and on the third side by the biblical text that I had promised to faithfully preach and teach. I was most at ease with the biblical text. When I had it all to myself, it was almost simple. But when I realized that as a pastor I would never again have it all to myself, that I was now exposed on the two other fronts of church and world, I knew that I was in over my head and needed help. The textual front required intelligence and attention, but I was used to that and enjoyed it. The congregational front was a surprise. These people were my friends and allies, but they were constantly interpreting my interpretations through filters of self-interest. I found that the Scriptures that I was preaching and teaching were being rewritten, unconsciously but constantly, in the minds of my parishioners to give sanction to behaviors and values that, more often than not it seemed to me, were in the service of the American way (in which indulgent consumerism was conspicuous) rather than the way of the cross (where sacrificial love was prominent). The large Sinai and fresh Galilee proclamations that I made on Sundays were coming back to me on weekdays in the reporting that people unconsciously provide in their confidences and small talk as stale bromides and puny moralisms. I had, it seemed, a vigorous cottage industry in miniaturization thriving in my congregation. Meanwhile, on the third front, the indifference of the world to what I was grandly calling the Kingdom of God put into question the validity of the whole enterprise. If I could be ignored so blithely and totally, could I be doing anything of significance? Barth helped me on every front in his commentary on Romans. He dove into the text, into these living waters, with abandon. He is such an exuberant exegete! It hardly mattered, I sometimes felt, whether he was right or wrong on a specific point; he was so patiently passionate with the text that it was at least safe from pedantry, a terrible fate. On the second front, the congregational, I found him page after page disentangling gospel spirituality from cultural religion, commending the former and rejecting the latter. All the subtle seductions to "another gospel" that I was noticing around me Barth had also but more discerningly noticed. How much well-meaning religious nonsense he saved me from! As for the world, Barth was immensely knowledgeable but quietly unintimidated. He knew politics and labor and prisons; but he believed in prayer and Scripture and the cross of Christ. Every rereading of Barth's *Romans* makes me less timid on the world front. Nobody in this century has done this better for me than Karl Barth.

9. Teresa of Avila, **THE COLLECTED WORKS**, translated by Kieran Kavanaugh, O.C.D., and Otilio Rodriguez, O.C.D. (1976). St. Teresa is completely unpretentious — an essential but rare quality in spirituality. She is profound, witty, playful, and honest. These three volumes immerse us in wide-ranging experience that is marked by a wonderful sanity.

10. John Calvin, **INSTITUTES OF THE CHRISTIAN RELIGION**, translated by John McNeill (1960). Spirituality includes the mind — the *thinking* mind, attempting to follow and respond to the mind of God as well as his heart. Calvin's heart was on fire, but his mind was clear. This is some of the keenest theology ever written, but written, every word of it, by a pastor in the middle of a parish of rather unruly sinner-Christians.

11. John Henry Newman, **APOLOGIA PRO VITA SUA** (1864). The brightest mind of nineteenth-century England was also a person of astonishing humility. By giving up just a little integrity he could have been the most honored and lauded Christian of the century; as it was he was mocked, vilified, and slighted — and hardly seemed to have noticed. Newman taught me never to expect applause or reward from either church or world for a life lived in pursuit of God.

12. William Foxwell Albright, **FROM THE STONE AGE TO CHRISTIANITY** (1945). Christian spirituality is formed in history: actual time, particular place, named people, specific language. It is at the outset neither an idea nor a feeling. Ideas and feelings are certainly honored and cultivated, but they do not come first. What comes first is God, the God who acts, who both makes and enters into this world in which we are born and die, eat and pray, work and play, make love and wage war. For over sixty years, Professor Albright discovered and recovered, observed and learned, studied and taught the immense array of data that makes up the conditions in which God's revelation takes place and our responses are worked out. Because most of the definitive revelation took place in the lands of the Middle East through the three millennia leading up to the incarnation of Jesus and was written in the Old and New Testaments, most of his attention was given to those times and places and writings, but there is hardly a detail anywhere or anytime that escapes his notice. He takes it all in, and with his wondrously generous and courteous mind/spirit renders it coherent to those of us who need all the help we can get in keeping our feet on the ground as we aspire to heaven. Albright is the person who, more than any other, has demonstrated for me both how spirituality is historically grounded and how scholarship works in the service of spirituality.

II

Classics

Familiarity with the classics is essential to being able to carry on intelligent conversations with our sisters and brothers in Christ. A few writers continue to be relevant generation after generation and across cultures. They keep us in touch with the areas of spirituality that everyone, it seems, at one time or another, has to negotiate. It matters little whether these books "appeal" to us right now — they are *there*. The giants in the land. We must rise to their level, and not habituate ourselves to companions of our small stature.

1. Thomas à Kempis, **THE IMITATION OF CHRIST**, translated by Ronald Knox (1959). This is not everyone's favorite, but it is on everyone's list. This is the most widely published and read book on spirituality in our tradition. It is amazing how well its medieval monkishness carries over into the modern world. When Dag Hammarskjöld was killed in an airplane crash in Africa, the two books in his briefcase were the Bible and the *Imitation*.

2. Ignatius Loyola, **THE SPIRITUAL EXERCISES**, translated by Thomas Corbishley (1963). Written by a soldier (or former soldier), this is a regimented and orderly sequence of guided meditations for one month. Its influence is vast. Meditation, always in danger of merely slipping into pious woolgathering, is put into a sturdy biblical harness and made to pull the imagination into prayer. There is much wisdom here capable of endless adaptation to different temperaments and situations.

3. THE CLOUD OF UNKNOWING, translated by E. Colledge and J. Walsh (1978). The fourteenth-century English writer of this unusual book is unknown. It is an immersion in what these days we are calling "left brain" discourse — an emptying of the mind of busy thoughts, a mind-shift into pure receptivity.

4. Blaise Pascal, **PENSÉES**, translated by W. F. Trotter (1941). In his century (the seventeenth), Pascal was one of the most brilliant scientists. A mathematician, he thought deep into the faith, searching, pondering. This meandering and unsystematic collection of brief thoughts (pensées) is modest but profound — a layperson's insistent search for the authentic and the experienced truth of God and spirit.

5. Pseudo-Dionysius, **COMPLETE WORKS**, translated by Colm Luibheid (1987). It's hard to believe, but this book, with the exception of the Scriptures themselves, has had more influence on Western spirituality than any other writing. Long thought to be written by Dionysius the Areopagite, the Athenian convert of Paul's preaching, it is now known to be written by a fifth-century Greek. Here is a mass transfusion of Neoplatonism into the bloodstream of Christianity. Some see this as enrichment, others as contamination. Either way it is *there*, and must be reckoned with.

6. Athanasius, **THE LIFE OF ANTONY**, translated by Robert C. Gregg (1980). This is an interesting contrast: Antony, whose intense, radical desert spirituality was a silent and solitary rebuke to soft, gossipy, Egyptian religion; and Athanasius, a pastor in a large and busy city, up to his ears in parish and politics, telling his story so that nondesert people can be influenced by Antony's courageous intentionality.

7. Bonaventure, **THE SOUL'S JOURNEY INTO GOD/THE TREE OF LIFE/THE LIFE OF ST. FRANCIS**, translated by Ewert Cousins (1978). Bonaventure does two things common in spirituality, but not often by the same person: he is a storyteller, giving us the story of St. Francis of Assisi, which continues to be creatively influential; and he is a mapmaker, sorting out, making diagrams, plotting schemes through the untidy and unruly terrain of pilgrimage toward God.

8. John Bunyan, **THE PILGRIM'S PROGRESS** (1684). This stunningly executed allegory has furnished the Christian imagination with names and situations that have now infiltrated most of our literature. Not often does something so popular manage also to be accurate.

9. Karl Barth, **EVANGELICAL THEOLOGY: An Introduction** (1963). Barth for me is *the* theologian of the twentieth century. He gathered up, rethought, repreached, and reprayed our entire Christian tradition. I would not want to be without even a page of his multivolumed *Church Dogmatics*. But this slim, spare book containing his final lectures, which he repeated in America, holds a special place in my reading. One reason is that I heard him deliver part of this book in person at Princeton. But another is that its "energetic brevity" (Barth's phrase) keeps the nature and necessity of theology forcefully focused in my life.

10. George Fox, **JOURNAL**, edited by Norman Penney (1924). Rejecting all authority, Fox subjected everything to the test of experience. His journal is instructive in the courage involved in such radical subjectivism, but also in the inevitable mistakes and errors that accompany it.

11. John of the Cross, **THE COLLECTED WORKS**, translated by Kieran Kavanaugh, O.C.D., and Otilio Rodriguez, O.C.D. (1979). Spiritual quest is bedeviled with fantasy and illusion because virtually everyone who pursues the spiritual life expects to be rewarded with ecstasy. John has no patience with what he calls our "spiritual sweet tooth." He is a ruthless realist, stripping away the illusions, the fantasies, and the delusions, guiding us through the consequent devastations, and training us to discern the realities of faith.

12. Bernard of Clairvaux, **SELECTED WORKS**, translated by G. R. Evans (1987). This twelfth-century abbot is one of the more impressive instances of the terrific energy and society-shaping activity that flows out of the contemplative life. Love is Bernard's theme, a non-sentimental, hardheaded and warmhearted love that is equally informed by self-knowledge and God-knowledge.

13. Søren Kierkegaard, **PURITY OF HEART** (1847). All institutionalized religion, all conventional religion, all veneer religion is trashed by Kierkegaard's sometimes caustic but always passionate writing. His diagnosis of the spiritual conditions of the Western world continues to probe church and Christian for signs of sluggish faith, of obese devotion.

14. THE PHILOKALIA, 3 volumes, compiled by St. Nikodimos of the Holy Mountain and St. Makarios of Corinth, translated and edited by G. E. H. Palmer, Philip Sherrard, and Kallistos

Ware (1979). This collection of texts, written over a period of a thousand years (between the fourth and fifteenth centuries), is our most authoritative access to the rich and vibrant spirituality of Eastern Orthodoxy (Greek and Russian). Because of cultural and historical divisions, most of us in the West have been ignorant of Orthodoxy. Our ignorance is impoverishment. An understanding and appreciation of the light-filled and passionately practiced prayer life on display in these pages is revitalizing.

15. Hans Urs von Balthasar, **THE GLORY OF THE LORD: A Theological Aesthetics**, 7 volumes (1982). Balthasar is the most comprehensive and penetrating of this century's writers in the field of spirituality. He is to prayer and spirituality what Barth is to theology — the Mountain. Virtually the entire Christian praying tradition is rethought and reprayed by this Swiss master.

III

The Psalms

The Hebrew Psalms were taken over by the Christian Church as our basic text for prayer. Christians have been praying them now for two thousand years, both corporately as we meet for worship and individually as we open our hearts to God in every place and circumstance. Nothing in Scripture or tradition rivals the Psalms as a holy and shaping influence on Christians at prayer.

The Psalms have also been prayerfully studied through the centuries by devout scholars. There are formidable difficulties, though, in *studying* a prayer text, for prayer requires a personal relationship in love, not the impersonal intellectual interrogation of a classroom. But as with all biblical (and ancient) texts, we need the help of scholars to get the most out of them, for they were composed in conditions and in a language remote from us. We have been most blessed by those scholars who join their intellectual acumen in the text with a passionate seeking after God in a way that stimulates us to both an understanding of and desire for God in prayer.

1. Dietrich Bonhoeffer, **PSALMS: The Prayer Book of the Bible** (1970). This minuscule book is major in its message. The experience of a praying lifetime is distilled in these brief chapters. Bonhoeffer recovered the practice of psalm-praying both for himself and for his age, as the martyr Christians of Germany dug down to the foundations.

2. John Calvin, **COMMENTARY ON THE PSALMS**, translated by James Anderson (1845). Calvin is a consistently brilliant commentator on Scripture, but he surpasses himself on the Psalms. These five volumes are mature reflection on the life of prayer as it is worked out in conversation with the Psalms and worked into experienced faith.

3. C. S. Lewis, **REFLECTIONS ON THE PSALMS** (1948). Here is a layperson *praying* the Psalms and reflecting on what he is doing. If we are ever intimidated by scholars or alienated by a remote language and culture as we come to the Psalms, Lewis's wonderful simplicity and unpretentious devotion sets us right. I read this and think, "Why, I could do that." Then I hear Lewis's answer, "All right, go ahead — do it."

4. Hans-Joachim Kraus, **COMMENTARY ON THE PSALMS** (1987). This may be the best long commentary from our century. It has recently been translated and so is accessible in English.

5. Arthur Weiser, **THE PSALMS** (1962). This is my choice for a scholarly, one-volume commentary. It offers solid, devout scholarship yet also appreciates the nature of worship and prayer.

6. A. F. Kirkpatrick, **THE PSALMS** (1957). The first edition of this commentary was published in 1902, and so it does not have up-to-date lexical data, but it is so accurate and succinct in what it does have that I find it a standard work still, and keep it close at hand. I can rarely put my finger on the actual evidence, but I nearly always feel that Kirkpatrick is not only studying the Psalms but also praying them.

7. Thomas Merton, **BREAD IN THE WILDERNESS** (1971). Here is the entire practice of praying the Psalms as it was developed and nurtured among the contemplative communities of monks and nuns from early times to the present. But this is not an historical study; it is a lived experience out of the living traditions.

8. Alexander MacLaren, **THE PSALMS** (1892). This is out of print, but if you like the Victorian commentators as much as I do, this will be worth looking out for in used bookstores. MacLaren, a British Baptist pastor, was among the best of the Victorians, and in the Psalms he is at his best.

9. William L. Holladay, **THE PSALMS THROUGH THREE THOUSAND YEARS: Prayerbook of a Cloud of Witnesses** (1994). I am always on the lookout for scholars who pray, theologians who pray, *Christians* who pray — companions in pilgrimage who are more interested in God than in the latest gossip from the library, sanctuary, or conference. Holladay is a scholar who prays: this book gathers a lifetime of scholarship in the Hebrew Scriptures into an invitation to take our place among our praying ancestors.

10. Walter Brueggemann, **THE MESSAGE OF THE PSALMS: A Theological Commentary** (1984). This is the best introduction to the Psalms as spirituality — the *experience* of God and difficulties with God. It is not a commentary in the strict sense, but provides an orientation in the nature of Psalm praying.

14

11. Claus Westermann, **PRAISE AND LAMENT IN THE PSALMS** (1981). In addition to being an excellent scholar of the text, Westermann deals with theological dimensions in such ways that our praying is connected with the larger context of God's ways of salvation.

12. Martin Luther, **LUTHER'S WORKS**, volumes 10-14, edited by Jaroslav Pelikan (1955-74). The rediscovery of experience as accessible to theology, one of Luther's primary contributions, was worked out in the Psalms and in Romans. Luther is not a "cautious" exegete, but extravagant, which I like very much.

IV

Prayer

Prayer is practiced out of a conviction that the genius of being human is the ability to be in communion with God. As that communion matures it gathers every detail of our lives — body, spirit, environment, relationships — into a God-animated aliveness, which is spirituality.

But *books* on prayer need to be picked up and read with some caution lest the book itself become a diversion, a distraction from the actual practice of prayer. Reading about prayer can easily become a lazy substitute for prayer. For prayer is not a subject; it is a form of existence.

All the same, books on prayer are useful in their place. Their place is not instruction, but companionship. It is encouraging to be in conversation with a few others who take prayer seriously, who engage in it faithfully, and who are willing to reflect honestly and wisely on what they do.

Any book that stimulates us or guides us to being attentive and responsive to God is in a sense a book on prayer. I have tried to provide a mix here of books about prayer and books that are acts of praying.

1. Frederick von Hugel, **THE LIFE OF PRAYER** (1921). This slim book, composed of two lectures, is weighty. Von Hugel is one of the twentieth-century masters in the spiritual life. (This also appears in *Essays and Addresses on the Philosophy of Religion*, 2nd series.)

2. Martin Buber, **I AND THOU**, translated by Walter Kaufmann (1970). Prayer is under constant danger of slipping into religious gossip, talking *about* God. Buber shows the genius of language as its capacity to address the person, the "Thou," and to answer as a Thou rather than an It.

3. Eugen Rosenstock-Huessy, **I AM AN IMPURE THINKER** (1970). Not a book strictly about prayer, but about language and the various ways we use and misuse it. I have learned as much indirectly from this German who immigrated to America, this Jew who converted to Christianity, than from most who write directly on prayer.

4. Friedrich Heiler, **PRAYER: A Study in the History and Psychology of Religion** (1932). A basic foundational work about prayer, providing a wealth of information and classification. Not so much a work that teaches or motivates us to pray, but rather one that orients us in the world in which people have prayed, and the ways they have prayed.

5. C. S. Lewis, **LETTERS TO MALCOLM: Chiefly on Prayer** (1964). Succinct wit, wise practice, and clear thinking character-ize this book. The split between intellect and spirit, so common in our world, is nowhere evident in Lewis, a person of immense learning who prayed as simply and as trustingly as a child.

6. Neville Ward, **THE FOLLOWING PLOUGH** (1978). I sometimes give this book to persons who are ready for "second helpings" — persons with a healthy and growing appetite for God. The style is casual and accessible; the contents are substantial.

7. Simon Tugwell, **PRAYER IN PRACTICE** (1974) and **PRAYER: Living with God** (1975). This pair of books by Tugwell, a British Dominican, is full of wise teaching rooted in centuries of Christian praying, and expressed cleanly. The tone is contemporary but there is nothing innovative here, nothing faddish — these are fresh blossoms issuing from old stock.

8. John Cassian, **CONFERENCES**, translated by Colm Luibheid (1985). Written by a monk for monks in the early fifth century, this is amazingly up-to-date as a book by a pastor for pastors. Cassian did what we are also trying to do — take the old traditions and rework them in a changed and changing world. Although this book is relatively obscure (except among Benedictines), I know of no one who hasn't responded to a first reading without saying something on the order of "Why didn't anyone tell me of this book before!"

9. P. T. Forsyth, **THE SOUL OF PRAYER** (1916). Prayer is the most personal thing that any of us do, the most human act in which we can engage. We are more ourselves, our true, image-of-God selves, when we pray than at any other time. That is the glory of prayer, but it is also the trouble with prayer, for these *selves* of ours have a way of getting more interested in themselves than in God. The plain fact is that we can't be trusted at prayer. Left to ourselves we become sel*fish* — preoccupied with our pious feelings, our religious progress, our spiritual standing. We need guides and masters to refocus our attention on God, to keep us ever mindful of the priority of God's word for us. We require an alert theologian at our right hand. Peter T. Forsyth is among the very best. He is a no-nonsense writer and pastor who goes for the jugular. In Forsyth's company we are aware of both the glory and the gravity of what we are doing when we go to our knees in prayer.

10. Jacques Ellul, **PRAYER AND MODERN MAN** (1973). A vigorous, energetic exploration of the nature of prayer understood and practiced in the cultural conditions of our age. We can never pray by archaeological findings — imitating our ancestors. We must always work it out in the context of this age. Ellul is a perceptive and penetrating guide.

11. Kenneth Leech, **TRUE PRAYER** (1980). This is basic, invitational instruction on prayer. Elemental but not elementary. Solid, mature writing.

12. Harry Emerson Fosdick, **THE MEANING OF PRAYER** (1915). I had a pastor when I was young who in the course of his sermons regularly denounced Fosdick as the enemy. It was the decade following the fundamentalist controversies, and my part of the Christian world viewed Fosdick as a leader of the opposition. And then one day in my young adulthood I met him. In the personal meeting there was no getting around the fact that this man was a Christian, a warm, convinced, unpretentious, and committed Christian. Sometime later I discovered this book of his on prayer and found it to be a true book of true prayer. And then one day in the course of reading and praying my way through it I realized that Fosdick had written this book, which was bringing thousands of men and women to their knees in prayer, at the very

time that he himself was being vilified by my pastor. I happen to think that my pastor was mostly right in his criticism of Fosdick's theology, even though the spirit in which he gave it was quite wrong. But I now wonder if my pastor would have spoken any differently if he had known that at the very moment that intemperate condemnations were raining down on him from pulpits all over the country, Fosdick was on his knees praying, devoutly and in the name of Jesus.

13. James M. Houston, **THE TRANSFORMING FRIEND-SHIP** (1989). Two sources provide substance to the practice of prayer. First and primarily, the biblical sources: Houston immerses us in exegetically rich and meditatively warm considerations of the biblical prayers: prophets and psalms, the praying of Jesus in the comprehensiveness of the Trinity, and the prayers of Paul. All this praying is understood in the context of friendship with each other and with God. The other source is the extensively praying Christian Church. He has made friends with people who pray and makes them our friends: Teresa of Avila and John of the Cross, Luther and Calvin, George Herbert and Francis de Sales. Since friendship is the metaphor that shapes our practice of prayer, it is obvious that anything that smacks of the technological is out of place. Friendships do not thrive on formulas or techniques; we have to *be* there, put ourselves in company with the other, and see what happens. We are dealing with innerness, something organic that must grow, not outerness that can be engineered. Houston gets us in touch with the totality of our innerness — temperament, personality, culture — and helps us realize this assembled wholeness as responsive to God.

14. Richard Foster, **PRAYER: Finding the Heart's True Home** (1993). Richard Foster takes us into the huge forest of prayer and names each tree, points out what is distinctive in each bush and flower. After a few hours in his company, the profusion of detail that at first overwhelmed and bewildered us now delights us, pulling us deeper into the forest. Foster is an expert and most courteous guide in all manner and kinds of prayer.

15. Alexander Whyte, **LORD, TEACH US TO PRAY** (1910). Whyte was an Edinburgh pastor who prayed as much and as well as he preached. Not all pastors pray. There is a great irony here: the very persons assigned responsibility in the Christian community for teaching and leading Christians in prayer are often personally prayerless. Whyte prayed. Immensely learned and energetic, he centered all his learning and energy in a life of prayer, suffused with a spirit of prayer.

V

Prayerbooks and Hymnbooks

I was reared in a tradition that scorned written and read prayers. Book prayers. Dead prayers. Reading a prayer would have been like meeting an old friend on the street, quickly leafing through a book to find an appropriate greeting suitable for the meeting and then reading, "Hello, old friend; it is good to see you again. How have you been? Remember me to your family. Well, I must be on my way now. Goodbye." And then closing the book and going on down the street without once looking my friend in the eye. Ludicrous. The very nature of prayer required that it be spontaneous and from the heart.

But along the way, I began to come across books of prayers that gave me words to pray when I didn't seem to have any of my own. I found that books of prayers sometimes primed the pump of prayer when I didn't feel like praying. And I found that, left to myself, I often prayed in a circle, too wrapped up in myself, too much confined to my immediate circumstances and feelings, and that a prayerbook was just the thing to get out of the brambles and underbrush of my ego, back out in the open country of the Kingdom, under the open skies of God.

In the process of discovering, to my surprise, alive and praying friends in these books, I realized that all along the prayers that had most influenced me were *written* (in the Bible), and that the lively and spirited singing we did in church was, for the most part, praying from a book, the hymnbook. My world of prayer expanded.

1. THE BOOK OF COMMON WORSHIP (1946). The church in which I have worshiped and served as pastor throughout my adult life (Presbyterian) has a book of prayers for the various occasions of worship. I have no sense that it is the best of the authorized denominational prayerbooks, but this was the one given to me and I have made it my own. It has been my primary text for leading others in prayer in thirty-five years of pastoral ministry, but it has also served as my own personal prayerbook. I like praying in words and phrases that I know have been used by hundreds of thousands of my ancestors, across many centuries, in uncounted congregations, on every continent.

2. John Baillie, **A DIARY OF PRIVATE PRAYER** (1949). I find a cadenced and austere beauty in these morning and evening prayers. And a searing honesty. There is always a temptation in written prayer toward rhetorical flourish, grandstanding before the Almighty. These prayers guide us in a way of prayer that is simple, direct, and immediate.

3. Jeremy Taylor, **THE GOLDEN GROVE**. My copy of this book, a gift from a friend, was printed in 1685 and inscribed by its first owner, "Mary Blaker, her book." Its subtitle is "What is to be Believed, Practiced and Desired or Prayed for; the Prayers being fitted to the several Days of the Week." Jeremy Taylor was a bishop in the Church of England during strife-ridden times; he composed this prayerbook, as he put it on the title page, "for the use of the Devout, especially of younger Persons." In encouraging and guiding Christians to pray, he was serving Christ best. Even though the language is antique, there is hardly a phrase that doesn't continue to strike a deep chord of urgency. True prayer never goes out of date.

4. David Head, **HE SENT LEANNESS: A Book of Prayers for the Natural Man** (1959). Our prayer masters counsel us to pray without inhibitions, speaking and shouting and crying whatever is in our hearts. God wants us to come to him just as we are, not as we should be. But that does not mean that we should persist in praying exclusively on grounds of sincerity. Sometimes our sincere prayers are quite wrongheaded and need to be set right. Not infrequently prayer needs purging of ignorance and selfishness. These prayers alert us to the kind of praying that needs training in the company of Jesus and Scripture.

5. David Adam, **THE EDGE OF GLORY: PRAYERS IN THE CELTIC TRADITION** (1985). We hope, as we pray, to be freed of the clutter and cacophony of the world. These spare, clean, and chiseled prayers help us to do that, help us to clear space for being simply ourselves before God.

6. John Oliver Nelson, editor, **THE STUDENT PRAYERBOOK** (1953). Prepared as a guide and encouragement in prayer for students, this prayerbook quickly transcended its target readership and became for many of us a means of staying in touch with a wide variety of "sorts and conditions" of prayers and pray-ers. The editor brought freshness and vitality to everything he did, and not least to this prayerbook.

7. Ernest T. Campbell, **WHERE CROSS THE CROWDED WAYS** (1973). These prayers were written and used to lead a congregation in prayers of Sunday worship. They are a wonderful fusion of the themes and diction that have been at the heart of Christian prayer for centuries, cast in the vocabulary and urgencies of a local congregation (Riverside Church, New York City) at a particular time (the 1970s).

8. **THE HYMNBOOK** (of the Presbyterian Church) (1955). The Psalms were the church's first hymnbook. But it was soon expanded to include ". . . hymns and spiritual songs" (Col. 3:16). Every generation of Christians adds new prayers to our corporate repertoire of sung prayers. It used to be common in Christian homes to have a hymnbook alongside the Bible for the use of family members, whether together or alone. It is a practice ripe for revival — it provides a vital link between Sunday praying at church and daily praying (whether said or sung) at home. The best hymnbook to have at home is the one you use in church on Sunday. This one is no better than others; it just happens to be the one I've used for most of my life.

9. Erik Routley, editor, **REJOICE IN THE LORD** (1985). Hymnals edited by committees have the advantage of meeting the needs of most of the people in a particular tradition, and so most denominations have such a hymnal. But this one by Scottish pastor Erik Routley brings the expertise and passion of a single heart and discriminating mind to its selection of hymns. That means that there are more surprises than usual. Routley provides a solid orientation in traditional hymnody, but he is alert also to the songs that the Spirit is inspiring today. Of all the solo-edited hymnals available, I like this one best.

10. **INTERVARSITY HYMNS** (1947). Much more so than in earlier centuries, twentieth-century Christian experience has

25

spilled out of its traditional ecclesiastical and denominational structures and found fresh forms of expression in mission and evangelism. As Christians from diverse backgrounds gather together, they always, of course, sing. The stimulus and initiative of these parachurch spiritualities has resulted in many a "new song." This hymnbook holds an honored place in respecting the hymns from the major worshiping traditions while staying alert to new songs.

VI

Worship/Liturgy

Common worship, the congregation gathered in worship on the Lord's Day, is the fundamental structure for the nurture of spirituality and the practice of prayer. But in North America we have experienced a century of subversive anti-worship: the sacred time and place have been subverted to religious entertainment, to the cultivation of pious narcissism, to a staging platform for messianic do-goodism. But the fundamental need is to attend to God. Christians are assigned the responsibility of meeting with their brothers and sisters regularly at a time and space set apart for that purpose, and that only. If we use this precious hour for other purposes, however well intentioned, we betray our friends, our community, and our calling.

The single most important thing I did for thirty-five years was stand before a congregation each Sunday morning and say, "Let us worship God." I loved doing that, loved the hours spent getting ready to do it, loved entering into the action that followed. And then my vocation took an unexpected turn and I wasn't doing it any longer.

What I've done for others all these years, I'm now having done for me — and how I do appreciate it. Every call to worship is a call into the Real World. You'd think that by this time in my life I wouldn't need to be called anymore. But I do. I encounter such constant and widespread lying about reality each day and meet with such skilled and systematic distortion of the truth that I'm always in danger of losing my grip on reality. The reality, of course, is that God is sovereign and Christ is savior. The reality is that prayer is my mother tongue and the eucharist my basic food. The reality is that baptism, not Myers-Briggs, defines who I am.

Very often when I leave a place of worship, the first impression I have of the so-called "outside world" is how small it is — how puny its politics, paltry its appetites, squint-eyed its interests. I have just spent an hour or so with friends reorienting myself in the realities of the world — the huge sweep of salvation and the minute particularities of holiness — and I blink my eyes in disbelief that so many are willing to live in such reduced and cramped conditions. But after a few hours or days, I find myself getting used to it and going along with its assumptions, since most of the politicians and journalists, artists and entertainers, stockbrokers and shoppers seem to assume that it's the real world. And then some pastor or priest calls me back to reality with "Let us worship God," and I get it straight again, see it whole.

1. Gregory Dix, **THE SHAPE OF THE LITURGY** (1945). If we need convincing that prayer is the Christian's main business, and that the liturgy is our primary means for engaging in it, this book should do it. No matter what tradition we are in, liturgical or nonliturgical, we need to know what tradition we came out of. This is both lively and comprehensive.

2. Howard G. Hageman, **PULPIT AND TABLE** (1962). I have never thought that there is one "best" way to worship. We do not worship on archaeological principles. Our biblical authorities do not instruct us on many of the details on which we need to make decisions and are distressingly vague on much of the rest. But that doesn't leave us free to shop for religious experience, browsing among the Quakers, the Baptists, and the Catholics for whatever suits our mood and inclination at the time. Worship is not a consumer activity; it is a sacrificial offering of our bodies to God (Rom. 12:1). However we worship, we must do it courteously in community and deliberately to the glory of God. "Courteously" and "deliberately" mean honoring the traditions in which we find ourselves. For me, this has meant understanding and feeling at home in the Reformed traditions into which I have been called as a worker in the vineyard. Howard Hageman, a Reformed pastor in Newark, New Jersey, has helped me to do that more than anyone else. This slim classic, written in the immediate context of parish ministry, but out of a lifelong immersion in the thinking and praying of our Reformed ancestors, has given me focus, orientation, and understanding to do my best in my time and place.

3. Rudolf Otto, **THE IDEA OF THE HOLY** (1923). This classic exploration of the sense of awe that permeates all reverential approaches to life is a grounding and orientation in the mystery that is all around us.

4. Mircea Eliade, **MYTHS, DREAMS, AND MYSTERIES** (1960). It helps, I think, to have an informed sense of the religious awe that is basic to the human being, as such. For it is out of that context that worship is shaped. There is nothing specifically Christian here, nothing that we would recognize immediately as the worship we conduct in our sanctuaries — but this is the world that revelation invades and out of which our Christian responses are made.

5. Annie Dillard, **TEACHING A STONE TO TALK** (1982). The long essay, "An Expedition to the Pole," is especially good. This is the best Christian account of what actually goes on in Christian worship that I have read — of what we are trying to do and why we fail every time.

6. Evelyn Underhill, **WORSHIP** (1936). A solid account of the world of worship first in its nature and then in its historical forms.

7. Bard Thompson, **LITURGIES OF THE WESTERN CHURCH** (1962). A selection of thirteen significant liturgies ranging from the second century to the eighteenth. This is the way some of our ancestors prayed when they gathered on the Lord's Day.

8. W. Nicholls, **JACOB'S LADDER: THE MEANING OF WORSHIP**, Ecumenical Studies in Worship, No. 4 (1958). Brief and on target. Written from the perspective of the pastor.

9. Wilhelm Hahn, **WORSHIP AND CONGREGATION**, Ecumenical Studies in Worship, No. 12 (1963). The context, congregation, is too often omitted in treatments of worship. Here it is front and center.

10. Max Thurian, **THE EUCHARISTIC MEMORIAL, Ecumenical Studies in Worship**, Nos. 7 and 8 (1960). Thurian is a founding brother of the Taize Community in France, a gathering of Protestant monks. He is one of the strongest and sanest voices in our century calling for a biblical and reformed liturgy.

11. Geoffrey Wainwright, **DOXOLOGY** (1980). A systematic theology from the perspective of worship. A compendious book, which is especially attractive to pastors, I think, since it is written from the place in which we do most of our work, the sanctuary.

12. Abraham Joshua Heschel, **THE SABBATH** (1951). This brilliant essay on the nature of the holiness of time lays down the substructure upon which worship takes place.

13. J. G. Davies, editor, **WESTMINSTER DICTIONARY OF WORSHIP** (1979). The standard reference work.

VII

Spiritual Formation

God the Holy Spirit conceives and forms the life of Christ in us. Our spirits are formed by Spirit — *that* is spiritual formation.

The primary language of spiritual formation is metaphorical, with the metaphors provided by biology: conception and birth, growth and maturity. Following the birth narratives of both John and Jesus, Luke uses the word "grow" to refer to both physical and spiritual growth: "And the child [John] grew and became strong in spirit . . ." (Luke 1:80); "And the child [Jesus] grew and became strong, filled with wisdom; and the favor of God was upon him" (Luke 2:40); "And Jesus increased in wisdom and stature, and in favor with God and man" (Luke 2:52). Paul uses the same language in addressing the Ephesian Christians: ". . . we are to grow up in every way into him who is the head, into Christ" (Eph. 4:15). The language suggests that biological and spiritual growth are analogous. What is visible in men and women as we develop from infancy to maturity has analogies to what is invisible in us as Christ is formed in us.

We commonly become interested in spiritual formation when

we realize that long after having completed our biological growth, we are still not "grown up," not mature. We find ourselves living lopsided, fragmented, and distracted lives, lurching from impulse to stimulus or stuck in some role or function. We find ourselves longing for a put-together life, integrated and wise, centered and whole. The classic Christian word for it is *holy*, a holy life.

And then we find that just as there are things that we do that assist or impair our biological formation (matters of nutrition, exercise, health care, schooling, socialization), so there are also things that we do that assist or impair our spiritual formation (matters of prayer and worship, repentance and commitment, the exercise of discernment and the acquisition of wisdom).

The critical words here are "assist or impair." Growth, both biological and spiritual (and the spiritual encompasses the biological) is a mystery, a huge mystery, intricate and complex — a work of the Holy Spirit. Most of what takes place we know very little about. Most of what goes on we can do very little about. Our part in spiritual formation is necessarily a very modest affair. We must never assume that we can manage or control it. If we try we will almost certainly be a party to deformation rather than formation.

But the alternative must not be neglect. It is necessary that we give careful attention to what we can appropriately do that will *assist* and not *impair* the formation of a mature life of Christ in ourselves and our friends. The little that we can do often makes an enormous difference.

Christians have traditionally understood spiritual formation as development in holiness — living a holy life. In recent decades psychology has rudely elbowed holiness out of the center and more or less taken charge. It has not, by and large, been a good thing for spiritual formation. When spiritual formation permits itself to be dominated by the behavioral sciences, it is inevitably secularized and individualized with occasional prayerful nods upwards for help in self-actualization. Narcissus on his knees.

So while I have learned, and continue to learn, much from the behavioral scientists (some of whom are included here), they are not my primary guides.

1. Karl Barth, **THE CHRISTIAN LIFE, CHURCH DOG-MATICS IV, 4, Lecture Fragments** (1981). The Lord's Prayer has traditionally provided the classic focus for the spiritual formation of Christians. Since it is the Holy Spirit who does the forming in spiritual formation, the one essential thing that we do is pray, submitting ourselves to the Spirit's formation. Barth was a theologian who prayed, and the praying is continuously woven in and out of his writings. This final volume of his *Church Dogmatics* was, fittingly, an exposition of the Lord's Prayer. It was left unfinished at his death — he made it through only the first two petitions, leaving the remainder for us to complete.

2. Werner Jaeger, **PAIDEIA: The Ideals of Greek Culture,** 3 volumes, translated by Gilbert Highet (1945). *Paideia* is the Greek word for the comprehensive and integrated education of the person and the community that today we commonly designate as spiritual formation. Even though there is nothing specifically Christian in this study (it ranges from Homer to Plato), this large and inclusive sense of shaping character and culture is foundational to Western civilization, and when we come to specifically Christian concerns in spiritual formation, it prevents us from conceiving of such concerns as a pious option or supplemental religious activity. Spiritual formation is foundational — it *lays* the foundations. The Greeks took these matters with great seriousness and along the way acquired much wisdom. These volumes provide a magisterial summation of the wisdom and practice of our ancestors at the very top of their form.

3. Gerhard von Rad, **WISDOM IN ISRAEL** (1972). The Hebrews are our immediate predecessors in all matters of spiritual formation. "Wisdom" in Israel meant skill in living in the revelation and presence of God. Set alongside Prophetic ministry (proclaiming/preaching God's revelation) and Priestly ministry (bringing people into God's presence), Wisdom ministry is concerned that we live well what has been revealed, that we live appropriately in the presence of God. If we are to engage in the practice of spiritual formation in step with the first generation of Christians, it is important that we become familiar with the practices and assumptions regarding the molding of character and the imparting of culture which they grew up with and continued, mostly without comment, in the formation of Christian spirituality.

4. Margaret R. Miles, **PRACTICING CHRISTIANITY: Critical Perspectives for an Embodied Christianity** (1990). Our predecessors in living out the Christian faith have much to teach us. We sit at their feet and learn from them. But admirable and wise as so many of them were, none was infallible. We have to learn to sift and evaluate. Instead of looking at what theologians said about the Christian life, Professor Miles looks at the manuals of actual devotional practice, carefully examining what those theologians did. She is warmly appreciative, but also coolly critical. She trains us in the kind of admiration that is not gullible, a mode of appreciation that is not imitative but finely discerning.

5. Henry Adams, **THE EDUCATION OF HENRY ADAMS** (1918). Adams poses an enigma. Here is a spiritual autobiography by a highly intelligent, acutely perceptive, and deeply religious person who lived in a so-called Christian nation and yet never became a Christian. What is there about Christian spiritual formation that eluded or escaped Adams? Or what is there about Adams that kept him from committing himself to what he almost certainly understood and approved? Adams is not the first to puzzle us in these ways, and he will not be the last.

6. James Loder, **THE TRANSFORMING MOMENT** (1981). Intensely personal, this book is experienced and written out of a life of teaching and thinking about spiritual formation. The theoretical, the practical, and the personal are integrated here in an uncommon way.

7. P. T. Forsyth, **THE CURE OF SOULS: An Anthology of P. T. Forsyth's Practical Writings,** edited by Harry Escott (1971). This is exuberant writing and zestful spirituality. One of the most quotable of spiritual masters, Forsyth anticipated with astonishing prescience the spiritual conditions in which we are working in these last years of the twentieth century. Practically everything that Forsyth wrote, whether theological or sermonic, touches on spiritual formation. This anthology brings out the high points.

8. William Law, **A SERIOUS CALL TO A DEVOUT AND HOLY LIFE**, edited by Paul Stanwood (1978). There is something austere and strenuous about this work that has always appealed to me. The appeal is not to imitate as such, for the culture and circumstances (eighteenth-century England) are forbiddingly remote. But the insistence that everything believed about God be at the same time lived out in daily prayer and service sets a standard from which I don't want to stray.

9. Stanley Hauerwas, **A COMMUNITY OF CHARACTER** (1981). Too often, discussion of how to live rightly before God disintegrates into arguments over moral dilemmas, trying to figure out what we do in *this* situation. Hauerwas sets our decisions in a much larger context where we have a chance at developing a new way of life, a life of moral/spiritual *character*, rather than simply carrying out a few more or less moral decisions.

10. William James, **VARIETIES OF RELIGIOUS EXPERI-ENCE** (1902). William James was one of the earliest and wisest of American philosophers/psychologists. Much has been learned about the psychological dimensions of spiritual formation since James, but no one has exceeded him in wisdom. One of the dangers that psychology poses to spirituality is reductionism — reducing spirituality to what can be measured and tested and explained. James doesn't reduce. He doesn't stuff spirituality into a small file drawer in the large cabinet of psychology.

11. Erik Erikson, **CHILDHOOD AND SOCIETY** (1950) and **YOUNG MAN LUTHER** (1962). Of all the behavioral scientists of our century, I have learned most from Erikson. He came to psychoanalysis after first being an artist. He then ranged from psychoanalysis into history and culture, trying to understand how the spiritual life comes into expression in the children and youth, the men and the women of the twentieth century.

12. Dietrich Bonhoeffer, **LIFE TOGETHER**, translated by John Doberstein (1954). During Germany's Nazi years, Bonhoeffer gathered a small theological community in Finkenwalde, where he attempted a total integration of prayer and study, theology and spirituality. This book is one of the results: a powerful witness along with wonderful insights into the necessity and nature of community in any true spirituality. Spiritual formation cannot be carried off by ourselves on our own terms.

13. H. C. J. Moule, **VENI CREATOR** (1902). I like sometimes to immerse myself in "Victorian" theology and spirituality — it is leisurely, meditative, learned, and, well, holy. Reading Moule we

are in the company of a mature person of God whom we can trust and admire.

14. Richard Foster, **CELEBRATION OF DISCIPLINE** (1978). Like a child exploring the attic of an old house on a rainy day, discovering a trunk full of treasure and then calling all his brothers and sisters to share the find, Foster has "found" the spiritual disciplines that the modern world stored away and forgot, and has excitedly called us to celebrate them.

15. Adrian van Kaam, **FORMATIVE SPIRITUALITY**, 4 volumes (1983-87). Father van Kaam, a Dutch priest who founded the Institute for Spiritual Formation at Duquesne University, is attempting to bring the entire field of spirituality and spiritual formation under rigorous academic scrutiny, carefully and exactly describing it in all its complexity. Nothing quite like this has ever been attempted before. Given the nature of spirituality, I am not sure whether such an approach is desirable, but it must be noted.

VIII

Spiritual Direction

The prayerful attention that we give to another person as a spiritual being and the accompanying prayerful conversation that develops out of it is called spiritual direction. All Christians do it, more or less, whether we give this name to it or not. We would do it a lot more if we knew how important it was, how much difference it makes, and the precious legacy we have in it. I have sometimes defined spiritual direction as what we are doing when we don't think we are doing anything — we are *there*, but out of the way, not in the Spirit's way, and used by the Spirit in ways we are not conscious of.

In an age in which so much of what we do is defined functionally in a job description, the gentle and unobtrusive art of simply being with another person in Spirit and in Truth (John 4:24) is much neglected. Recovery and cultivation of this ancient Christian art is essential if we are to counter the devil's work of depersonalizing and merchandising the gospel.

Other forms of Christian discourse, such as preaching, teaching, and giving witness, have a much higher profile and are capable of clearer definition. In contrast, spiritual direction is modest work and does not call attention to itself. It is therefore easy to miss it or to devalue it. By watching/reading the masters at work, we come to appreciate how important it is to learn and practice this art.

1. Frederick von Hugel, **LETTERS TO A NIECE** (1928). Here is a master at work. Absorb the spirit and counsel in these letters and you will have the rudiments, and more, of spiritual direction.

2. Aelred of Rievaulx, **SPIRITUAL FRIENDSHIP**, translated by Mary Eugenia Laker, S.S.N.D. (1974). The human component in spiritual direction is simple friendship. Except that friendship is not simple. It is a highly complex and demanding kind of intimacy. This twelfth-century work by the abbot of a monastery in northern England holds both the complexities and the necessities before us for prayerful attention.

3. Francis de Sales, **INTRODUCTION TO THE DEVOUT LIFE** and **LETTERS OF SPIRITUAL DIRECTION**, translated by Peronne Marie Thibert (1988). Specifically directed to a spirituality of the laity in the context of workshop, bedroom and kitchen, and marketplace. There is always a tendency to think that really first-class prayer takes place in protected sanctuaries. This is a detailed refutation of that supposition, reinstating the devout life in the context of the secular and common world. (Incidentally, Francis's bishop sent him to Geneva to try to get Theodore Beza, John Calvin's associate, back into the Roman fold. He was unsuccessful.)

4. Samuel Rutherford, **LETTERS** (1891). Banned from his pulpit by political authorities, this seventeenth-century Scottish pastor wrote letters to friends and parishioners that probe the heart and expand the spirit. Search used bookstores for this one and read it for the treat of your life.

5. Kenneth Leech, **SOUL FRIEND** (1977). This is an attempt to recover the whole dimension of spiritual direction for those who have lost touch with it. A basic primer in the field. The finest treatment, I think, at an introductory level.

6. Martin Thornton, **SPIRITUAL DIRECTION** (1984). Thornton works out of an Anglican milieu. His strength is in his no-nonsense, straightforward, lay-it-on-the-table approach. A good antidote to the soupy, sentimental gushers who always seem to manage, sooner or later, to get into these discussions.

7. Thomas Merton, **SPIRITUAL DIRECTION** (1960). Another angle on the subject: working out of his Trappist monastery, Merton assimilates the contemplative traditions and brings them into the American present.

8. Pierre Teilhard de Chardin, **THE DIVINE MILIEU** (1960). The elements of spiritual direction are laid out here in a wonderful way by establishing the broadest and deepest context possible. Teilhard was a French Jesuit, professionally a paleontologist, and did his major scientific work in China. He was adept at crossing boundaries and making connections.

9. Gerald May, **CARE OF MIND/CARE OF SPIRIT** (1982). Spiritual direction is frequently confused with psychological counseling. Here they are separated. The writer is a psychiatrist and knows that field well; but he left that work to become a spiritual director. He knows the difference between psychology and spirituality and disperses some of the fog that confuses them.

10. Jerome Heufelder and Mary Coelho, editors, **WRITING ON SPIRITUAL DIRECTION BY GREAT CHRISTIAN MASTERS** (1982). This is an excellent anthology that ranges across the centuries and through the traditions.

11. Francis W. Vanderwall, S.J., **SPIRITUAL DIRECTION: An Invitation to Abundant Life** (1981). Brief, personal, and anecdotal. Not a classic by any means, but useful as a contemporary witness of a person who has taken personal steps to recover this practice and put it into practice.

12. Douglas V. Steere, **TOGETHER IN SOLITUDE** (1982). Not strictly on spiritual direction, but written by one of the master spiritual directors of our century. Steere is a Quaker. Everything he is and writes is an aspect of spiritual direction whether he is intending it or not.

13. Ralph Harper, **ON PRESENCE** (1991). The most important things about ourselves are not the most obvious. We are constantly, relentlessly externalized by both our culture and our friends, distracted from who we are. And so we require counter influences. Harper is wonderfully insightful and percipient in calling back into our awareness the presence and being present without which we cannot be with another.

14. Martin Luther, **LETTERS OF SPIRITUAL COUNSEL**, translated by Theodore Tappert (1955). Since spiritual direction is not the wholesale application of general principles, but the painstaking working out of spirituality in specific situations, the personal letter is one of its best expressions. Luther knew the holy gospel and the human heart, and the double knowledge is evident on the pages of these letters.

IX

North American Spirituality

Each culture carries with it spiritual assets and liabilities. Cultures of other languages, centuries, and histories offer unique insights into spirituality, but they also display blind spots. The Platonism of Augustine's age, for instance, provided a large intellectual framework that helped communicate the faith to the pagan mind and at the same time blunted, for the unwary, the sharp particularities of the cross and all its attendant materialism. Similar "double-entry bookkeeping" can be done on the Aristotelianism of the Middle Ages, on post-Reformation Calvinism, and on Enlightenment romanticism. Each age requires discernment to embrace its gospel-generated energies and truths and to avoid repeating its culture-conditioned errors. North American spirituality has its own flavor, requiring a trained palate to discern the best from the worst. Not all the writers I am listing are explicitly Christian, but they are all friendly to Christian convictions. I have selected these because each has seemed to have tapped into something that is characteristically North American.

1. Ann Morrow Lindberg, **GIFT FROM THE SEA** (1955). A penetrating account of a homemaker/mother/wife who goes to the seashore for a few days and finds metaphors among the seashells that connect the presence of God and the meaning of the soul in the traffic of her everyday housewife world.

2. Flannery O'Connor, **THE HABIT OF BEING** (1979). This edited collection of letters reveals the personal dimensions of deep spirituality. O'Connor died young (about forty) of the debilitating disease of lupus, and is deservedly best known for her extravagantly grotesque stories of God and grace among Americans. The letters show us what she was thinking and praying during the years she was creating and dying.

3. Henri J. M. Nouwen, **REACHING OUT: The Three Movements of the Spiritual Life** (1975). Nouwen is a Dutch priest who has become an American. A prolific writer, he has a great passion for entering into the thick of life, experiencing everything possible to experience, and then reporting back to us on his encounters with God.

4. Thomas Merton, **SEVEN STOREY MOUNTAIN** (1978). Merton's conversion from the freewheeling life of a young New York intellectual to Christ, followed by his entrance into the Trappist monastery of Gethsemane in Kentucky, became, by our Lord the Spirit, the most abundant source of freshly articulated spiritual writing in our century. This is not Merton's best book, but it is the story behind what later became his best writing.

5. Frederick Buechner, **THE SACRED JOURNEY** (1982), **NOW AND THEN** (1983), and **TELLING SECRETS**. Spiritual autobiography is notoriously difficult to write honestly; it is so tempting to gild the lily when writing about yourself and God.

44

Buechner "listens to his life" and tells his "inside" story without pretense and without varnishing the dull spots. Buechner, a Presbyterian, does some of his best spiritual writing in his novels.

6. Robert Pirsig, **ZEN AND THE ART OF MOTORCYCLE MAINTENANCE** (1974). This is spirituality in the form of a pilgrimage story through the West, with undertones of mental illness and overtones of growing up. A book of much wisdom, probing, and struggling for realization in everyday life. This is quite definitely not Christian spirituality; its usefulness comes from initiating a dialogue between the best that our culture produces more or less on its own, and the revelation that Jesus brings to us. (If you can find it, get the edition with the new 1984 introduction.)

7. Annie Dillard, **PILGRIM AT TINKER CREEK** (1974). This is mystical theology at its unpretentious best. Dillard is an exegete of creation in the same way John Calvin was an exegete of Holy Scripture. She brings to muskrats and mockingbirds the passion and intelligence that Calvin brought to Moses, Isaiah, and Paul. Dillard reads the book of creation with the care and intensity of a skilled textual critic, probing and questioning, teasing out, with all the tools of mind and spirit at hand, the author's meaning.

8. Virginia Stem Owens, **WIND RIVER WINTER**. An immersion in and reflection on the experience of death. The writer and her husband lived for a winter in a cabin in the Wyoming Rockies. She watches the world die, the snows and ice come, the below-zero winds chase everything living below ground or down south. She herself is "dying" — her husband's vocation is in crisis, her daughters are no longer "daughters" but grown women, obituaries of friends' marriages arrive through the postal service, a close friend dies, a stranger is killed. Deaths vocational, emotional, natural, and physical. Natural and unnatural death. Sudden and

lingering death. Owens avoids none of it. She whitewashes none of it. She embraces and accepts and receives. And spring arrives. This is a journal of one person's desire to "enter into that absolute still center at the heart of the universe, the death of Christ, where I could leave everything behind."

9. Walker Percy, **LOST IN THE COSMOS** (1983). These essays on culture, language, and the Christian faith combine the diagnosis of a novelist's imagination with the faith of a passionate Christian. Percy understands the desperate condition that we are in, and cares enough to do something about it.

10. Henry Thoreau, **WALDEN** (1854). Thoreau is an Elijah-like figure, a wilderness prophet, fiery and simple. He clears the clutter from our minds and spirits, slowing us down, silencing the gossip within us.

11. Ivan Doig, **THIS HOUSE OF SKY** (1978). Our present has a past — a past full of imperfections and inadequacies that is the stuff out of which present holiness is made. Understanding and appreciating this past, dealing with our parents and home, the way and place and circumstances of our rearing, is an essential dimension of spirituality. Doig does this impressively well in his honest, courageous, and affectionate memoir, with neither cynicism nor sentimentalism, the ditches into which such attempts often fall.

12. A. W. Tozer, **PURSUIT OF GOD** and **KNOWLEDGE OF THE HOLY** (1948). Here is a pastor who stuck to his post (in Chicago for forty years) and prayed and wrote with an evangelical fervor wedded to a catholic wisdom. This is unabashed piety, American style, integrated into centuries of insight and tradition.

13. John Woolman, **JOURNAL** (1774). Simplicity and beauty mark the spirituality of this Quaker tailor and shopkeeper, along with a quiet social passion for the disadvantaged. Woolman worked extensively in travel and speech on behalf of slaves and Indians. But he never neglected his own heart in the work.

14. Madeleine L'Engle, **THE CROSSWICKS JOURNALS** (1980). Most readers know L'Engle best through her many novels; I met her first in these journals and was captured by her honesty and Christian rootedness. It is to these journals that I return to cultivate friendship with a writer with the strongest of commitments — yet innocent of pretensions — to writing as a Christian vocation.

15. Dorothy Day, **THE LONG LONELINESS** (1952). Day began her working life as a journalist full of Marxist passion for exploited workers and for the poor. Then she was converted to the Christian way. She continued her working life as a journalist, but now with Christ's passion for the very same people — the exploited, the homeless, the poor. Her tabloid, *The Catholic Worker,* sold for a penny a copy, and articulated a Christian social conscience and action worked out on the streets of New York City. Day embodied a spirituality and a life of prayer in which deep personal piety and radical social/political action were inseparable.

X

Novelists

Novelists work the same field in which Christians pray, believe and obey, plowing and sowing and harvesting all the interconnections of ordinary lives. This statement by John Updike supports my conviction that the novel is an essential component in spiritual reading: "Fiction is nothing less than the subtlest instrument for self-examination and self-display that mankind has invented yet. Psychology and X-rays bring up some portentous shadows, and demographics and stroboscopic photography do some fine breakdowns, but for the full *parfum* and effluvia of being human, for feathery ambiguity and rank facticity, for the air and the iron, fire and spirit of our daily moral adventure there is nothing like fiction: it makes sociology look priggish, history problematical, the film media two-dimensional, and the National Enquirer as silly as last week's cereal box. . . . In fiction everything that searchers for the important tend to leave out is left in."

World conditions, a steady and relentless drizzle of acid rain, strip us of story, identity, and place. But it is the *story* of salvation for specific *people* in a particular *place* that composes the conditions of Christian spirituality. If we are rendered storyless and addressed as "Occupant" in "Anywhere," the distinctiveness of the Christian life is rubbed out. Meanwhile any number of fiction writers work away day after day, year after year, countering these world conditions, showing the story-shape of all existence, insisting on the irreducible identity of each person and the glory of this piece of geography.

Anyone, I think, serious about these elemental conditions of story, person, and place in which our salvation is worked out will welcome novelists as friends, and seek to spend time in their company. Not all writers of fiction, of course, qualify as allies. Discernment must be exercised, but a considerable number take their stand with us against the spirituality-debilitating conditions of the world.

1. Fyodor Dostoyevsky, **THE BROTHERS KARAMAZOV** (1879-80). Frederick Buechner has described this novel as "That great seething bouillabaisse of a book. It's digressive and sprawling, many too many characters in it, much too long, and yet it's a book which, just because Dostoyevsky leaves room in it for whatever comes up to enter, is entered here and there by maybe nothing less than the Holy Spirit itself, thereby becoming, as far as I'm concerned, what a religious novel at its best can be — that is, a novel less *about* the religious experience than a novel the reading of which *is* a religious experience: of God, both in his subterranean presence and in his appalling absence." The 1990 translation by Richard Devear and Larissa Volokhonsky is best.

2. Walter M. Miller, **CANTICLE FOR LEIBOWITZ** (1959). We live in an apocalyptic age — that seems clear enough. But if we are not careful the pressures of the apocalyptic mood can drive us into antispiritual cul-de-sacs — escapism or alarmism. Here is a story that trains us to live sanely and stubbornly as custodians of the faith in the midst of disaster, whether actual or incipient.

3. George Eliot, **MIDDLEMARCH** (1871-72). When I was only a few months a pastor, an older friend was astonished that I had never read this long, Victorian novel. So I read it. He was right to have been astonished at my illiteracy. The tangle of spiritual intimacy and vocational pride that is the worm in the apple of the Christian life is diagnostically narrated here in an unforgettable story.

4. George Bernanos, **DIARY OF A COUNTRY PRIEST**, translated by Pamela Morris (1937). The first and second times I read this, I thought it was a true story, and knew that I had a standard of integrity to live up to. When I later learned that the book was fiction, I was surprised but not disappointed. The sense of truth, if anything, deepened.

5. James Joyce, **ULYSSES** (1922). This story of an ordinary Jew living through the twenty-four hours of an ordinary day in a most ordinary city, Dublin, is rendered mythic: behind every episode there is the foundational story of Ulysses. This is an example of the power of story to yield the meaning of what might well go unremarked otherwise, but with one difference: it is the gospel story of Jesus, not the Greek myth of Ulysses, that we see being worked out in our lives and in the lives of our friends and neighbors. But Joyce shows us the method.

6. Herman Melville, **MOBY DICK** (1851). Our whole country is under the spell of Emersonianism, the sunny optimism that assumes everything will turn out all right if we just take ourselves seriously and think profound thoughts. Melville throws a monkey-wrench into the delicately meshed gears of transcendentalism by insisting that there is evil to deal with, and evil of huge dimensions, encountered in both human form (Captain Ahab) and in nature (the whale, Moby Dick). There is more to this business of spirituality than sunshine and the Oversoul; there is also the devil and all his angels.

7. Graham Greene, **THE POWER AND THE GLORY** (1940). Does anyone take with full seriousness the sheer power and glory into which ordination pulls us? In the spiritual climate of our day it tends to something tame along the lines of a career with benefits. But Greene takes ordination seriously, and his portrayal of the whiskey priest etches something vocationally numinous into our imaginations.

8. C. S. Lewis, **TILL WE HAVE FACES** (1956). It is a commonplace in spirituality that we have to become that which we wish to see or hear or receive. But it is a commonplace commonly ignored. This story makes it hard to ignore it ever again.

9. J. R. R. Tolkien, **THE FELLOWSHIP OF THE RING** (1965). Tolkien, a Catholic Christian, absorbed and assimilated all the old Icelandic and Teutonic myths and retold them in a Christian accent in this vast and marvelous story.

10. Anne Tyler, **SAINT MAYBE** (1991). Each new novel by Tyler is a fresh exercise in seeing behind the labels and clichés that stereotype people and prevent us from seeing the "image of God" that is there. She creates characters in her novels that are always just a little quirky, not quite fitting into what we think a human being ought to be. Most of us are so used to fitting into the categories supplied for us by hospitals, schools, shopping malls, and social services that we raise no objections when we are treated similarly by other Christians, and especially by Christian leaders. But insofar as we acquiesce, we lose the capacity to realize what God is most interested in working in us: sanctity, which means becoming more our created/redeemed selves, not less, not being reduced to what will fit into a religious program, not being depersonalized in the cause of ecclesiastical efficiency.

11. Walker Percy, **THE SECOND COMING** (1980). If Kierke-gaard lived today and chose the novel as his writing form, it might read like this. Percy combines several interests that are also at the heart of pastoral spirituality: care for language, curiosity in the ways truth is perceived and lived, God, a searing and comic criticism of anti-gospel religion.

12. Sigrid Undset, **KRISTEN LAVRANSDATTER** (1929). Undset, a convert in midlife to the faith, has fit most of what she knows of sin and salvation into the immensities of one woman's life in medieval Norway.

13. Walter Wangerin, Jr., **THE BOOK OF THE DUN COW** (1978) and **THE BOOK OF SORROWS** (1989). This pair of novels provides a penetrating insight into the world of sin and evil in which salvation does its work. Written in the form of a bestiary — a rooster, a flock of hens, and assorted other animals — the novels draw us via our imaginations into the complex world of salvation, and give us solemn warning that we can never, *never*, take the work of salvation into our own hands. Wangerin is in the very front rank of contemporary storytellers.

14. Rudy Wiebe, **THE BLUE MOUNTAINS OF CHINA** (1970). Rudy Wiebe specializes in Mennonites, a hardy form of Christian that has been much abused — a kind of Christian "Jew," often exiled but never defeated. But Mennonites are not well known across the spectrum of Christian denominations. Although fictional, this story renders the truth of Mennonite endurance, persecution, and survival-in-community in Germany, Russia, the Ukraine, Canada, and Paraguay. Mennonites, vehemently counter-cultural Christians, continue to leaven world and church, and this novel shows how they do it.

15. Robertson Davies, **THE DEPTFORD TRILOGY** (1985). For fifty years Davies has been writing novels that set mature spiritual wisdom in a North American context that is rife with spiritual ignorance and foolishness. We are fortunate to have this sagacious master's careful rendering of the kinds of lives that most of us are given to deal with (in ourselves and others) through these dark decades. Anything this Toronto writer writes is worth reading; this sequence of novels provides a solid center from which to range for instruction and delight.

16. Wallace Stegner, **THE BIG ROCK CANDY MOUNTAIN** (1945). Stegner has served as one of the premier storytellers in and for my life. I grew up in the West in a kind of anarchist/populist atmosphere. We sat loose to authority and had no sense of continuity with the past. The town in which I grew up was only forty years old when I arrived in it. I had no sense of tradition. The Scandinavia of my grandparents was half a world away, and the Kootenai and Salish Indians native to my valley were not ancestors in any living sense. People moved around a lot, looking for a "better deal." My family moved ten times during my childhood. Experiences were intense and sometimes glorious, but they weren't part of anything large or historic, and my understanding of the gospel was thereby reduced to the temporary and the "better deal." In this novel, Stegner makes a story out of the materials of my life. He grew up only a couple of hundred miles from me, but thirty years earlier, in a town not unlike mine. As I read his novel about the American/Canadian West and its people, I recognized in it most of the people I grew up with, and also the feelings I had, the language I learned and used, the wanderlust and loneliness, the rootless and religionless poverty/posterity. As an adult, I was in danger of rejecting it all in favor of something more congenial to what I understood as a *Christian* culture. Stegner's storytelling put the materials of my experience, the land and weather, the slang and customs, the jerry-built towns and makeshift jobs, into a story. He made a cosmos out of it, showed this country and people as capable of plot and coherence as anything in Homer's Greece or Mark's Galilee.

XI

Poets

Poets are natural allies to Christian pilgrims, and we need to cultivate their company. We who use words so much in witness, in preaching and teaching, conversing and praying, need to *care* for words — not let them be reduced to mere conveyors of information. Poets are the world's primary custodians of this complex intricacy of sound, rhythm, and meaning that occurs whenever we open our mouths and speak.

More than half of our Scriptures were written by poets. If the form in which something comes to us is significant — and it is — then poetry and poets are a force to be reckoned with for anyone who has responsibility in listening and giving witness to the "Word made flesh."

The first thing that a poet does is to slow us down. We cannot speed-read a poem. A poem requires rereading. Unlike prose, which fills the page with print, poems leave a lot of white space, which is to say that silence takes its place alongside sounds as significant, essential to the apprehension of these words. We cannot be in a hurry reading a poem. We notice connections, get a feel for rhythms, hear resonances. All this takes time. There is a lot to see, to feel, to sense. We sit before a poem like we sit before a flower and attend to form, relationship, color. We let it begin to work on us. When we are reading prose we are often in control, but in a poem we feel like we are out of control. Something is going on that we cannot pin down right away and so often we get impatient and go read Ann Landers instead. In prose we are after something, getting information, acquiring knowledge. We read as fast as we can to get what we want so that we can put it to good use. If the writer is not writing well — that is, if we cannot understand her quickly — we get impatient, shut the book, and wonder why someone does not teach her to write a plain sentence. But in poetry we take a different stance. We are prepared to be puzzled, to go back, to wait, to ponder, to listen. This attending, this waiting, this reverential posture, is at the core of the life of faith, the life of prayer, the life of worship, the life of witness. If we are in too much of a hurry to speak, we commit sacrilege. Poets slow us down, poets make us stop. Read it again, read it again, read it again.

1.   Dante, **THE DIVINE COMEDY**, translated by Dorothy Sayers (1949-62). There are occasional moments when a culture, the church, and an individual person converge in such a way that everything comes together with a sense of wholeness, completion. This is one of those occasions. Virtually everything that goes into the making of spirituality — the distortions, the failures, the trials, the achievements, the blessings — are arranged and ordered, put into rhythms and metaphors, and then narrated in such a way that we can see where our experience fits into the whole. This is also the most extensive analysis of sin, especially spiritual sin, that we have.

2.   John Milton, **PARADISE LOST** (1667). Spirituality is primarily about God; secondarily it is about sin. For all our seeking

or being sought by God takes place in an environment of the most subtle seductions to defy or evade God. Milton's imagination gets behind the appearances of morality and exposes the complex subtleties of negative spirituality, the antispirituality that is constantly at work undermining and eroding God-obedience, God-seeking, God-receiving. Christians need to be learned in this subject, and Milton is a good master.

3. Gerard Manley Hopkins, **POEMS**, edited by W. H. Gardner (1967). Hopkins, a British Jesuit, struggled mightily to integrate his priestly vocation and his poetic gifts. The poems that issue from this struggle are dazzling both in language and spirituality. I am always on the lookout for Christian friends who take words with a seriousness comparable to that with which they serve the Word. Hopkins does this so well.

4. William Carlos Williams, **PATERSON** (1963). This relentless and unembarrassed verbal attentiveness to ordinary persons in an ordinary town during ordinary days is a corollary to what Christians do with their lives. Williams was a physician of the old-fashioned school, making house calls, immersing himself in neighborhood, paying attention to pieces of broken glass and scraps of conversation, and scribbling his attentiveness into poems. Williams was not a practicing Christian — he practiced a kind of secular spirituality — but the thoroughness and humility of his poems is spiritually healthy.

5. Luci Shaw, **POLISHING THE PETOSKEY STONE** (1990) and **WRITING THE RIVER** (1994). These poems are a generous workshop in the operations of sanctity. I have been carrying around one thin book after another of Luci Shaw's poems for years, reading them, letting them be read to me — watching, listening. I use them for environmental protection: they filter noise out of the air so I hear quiet sounds breathing creation into being each morning; they scrub crude-oil grime from the landscape so I see contours in faces and fields and furniture that are containers for grace. The sights and sounds were there all the time, but habit and cliché and hurry obscured them. The poems whisper "holy, holy, holy" *here, now.* Before I know it and without moving an inch, I have stepped into sacred space, sacred time. I am a participant in just a little more reality (sometimes a lot more) than before.

6. Marianne Moore, **COLLECTED POEMS** (1951). These poems are delicately crafted artifacts, holding energetically robust truths. Though they never mention God, they are always about him — the wrestling of messy chaos into meticulous order, perceiving the lineaments of salvation under the cover of jerboas and steamrollers. Miss Moore's brother was a Presbyterian pastor and she regularly worshiped in his Brooklyn congregation.

7. Richard Wilbur, **POEMS** (1963). For sheer dexterity and dazzle, nothing I know compares to Wilbur. But there is far more: the creation as *creation* is appreciated and celebrated. And the task of being human as a task involving value and choice and affirmation is mapped.

8. William Stafford, **STORIES THAT COULD BE TRUE: New and Collected Poems** (1977). The simplicity and accuracy of Stafford's poems are a continual rebuke to my congenital tendencies to evangelical exaggeration and sermonic booziness. Reality (if it is in fact reality and not illusion) doesn't need varnish. God (if this is in fact God and not an idol) doesn't need hype.

9. John Donne, **THE HOLY SONNETS** (1635). An Anglican priest in seventeenth-century London, Donne was a contemporary of George Herbert (whom I have listed under "Basics"). But he is very different from Herbert. Whereas Herbert is quiet and modest, working the terrain of the ordinary parish, Donne is dramatic and fiery, tackling the big issues in the big city, confronting dragons and death.

10. Emily Dickinson, **COLLECTED POEMS**, edited by Thomas H. Johnson (1960). The great value of Dickinson's poems for me is that they come at the spiritual life obliquely. There is a kind of shy indirection here, which slips past cliché and overfamiliarity, and shakes out stale pieces of experience for fresh perception.

11. Jack Leax, **REACHING INTO SILENCE, THE TASK OF ADAM, COUNTRY LABORS**. These are poems of evangelical austerity, a spirituality that works close to the bone. A poetry of elementals: pain, earth, trees, woodsmoke, flesh.

12. Czeslaw Milosz, **COLLECTED POEMS** (1990). The wonder of Milosz is his capacity to embrace our entire century in his poems. And what a century it has been — a century of devastation, exile, secularization, disillusionment, rootlessness, confusion. A cruel century, most of which has entered his own soul. All this and more Milosz tends to in these poems, but without raising his voice, without straining for effects. And without losing his faith in Jesus as sovereign and savior. His witness is all the more impressive for being stated so modestly, so unassumingly.

13. Margaret Avison, **SELECTED POEMS** (1991). Avison is one of God's spies. She works her way through territory claimed by the world, the flesh, and the devil and discovers details of beauty and grace and truth all over the place. Details of God. I have found Avison to be one of Canada's best poets.

14. T. S. Eliot, **THE FOUR QUARTETS** (1943). Eliot established his reputation as the spiritual diagnostician of the twentieth century with his long poem, *The Waste Land*. But if the *Waste Land* is the diagnosis, *The Four Quartets* is the cure. Eliot manages to get most of the life of prayer and spirituality compressed and imaged in these poems.

15. W. H. Auden, **FOR THE TIME BEING** (1944). I read this "Christmas Oratorio" every Advent, and let Auden's imagination stretch my own to make connections between Bethlehem and Bel Air (the town in which I lived for thirty years). The wonderful thing about Auden is that he believes the Christian story absolutely, but also believes that it is continuously contemporary, and is able to say it again in our idiom.

XII

Pastors

If I had been a nurse or a scientist or a plumber or a lawyer, this section would deal with the men and women who worked out their spirituality in one of those vocations. But for most of my vocational life, I have been a pastor in a single-pastor church. As such, my primary associations have been with engineers, homemakers, truck drivers, schoolteachers, lawyers, merchants, stockbrokers, grocery clerks, nurses, physicians, farmers, and carpenters — which is to say, men and women who are *not* pastors. Since work conditions are a huge factor in our spirituality, I have given much attention to helping my parishioners work out their Christian identity and behavior within the particular conditions of their workplace. One of the ways I did that was to encourage them to meet or read about others who had lived their faith in similar vocational circumstances. In the midst of that I realized that no one was helping me deal with the particular tensions, temptations, and dynamics of being a Christian in *my* workplace. I figured I had better do for myself what I was encouraging in others.

61

What do pastors do? Really do? The ones who have done it best? Spirituality — this life of passion and God — is no harder for pastors than for engineers or carpenters or fastfood cooks or homemakers. But the "conditions" are unique, and so the responses require adequate dealing with conditions. The life of prayer, which is to say, life lived authentically and passionately and creatively, is at particular risk among pastors, for so much in the daily work provides public, but spurious, substitutes for it. I have sought out pastors who have done this well and have then kept company with them, learning from them, being rebuked by them, finding hope in my own poverty and congregational wasteland by entering through imagination and prayer into what I can learn of their stories. These are the ones who have been of particular help in protecting me from the malign influence of religious celebrities and keeping me at my last.

1. Alexander Whyte, **BUNYAN CHARACTERS IN PILGRIM'S PROGRESS.** The twin pillars of pastoral life are prayer and learning. The two are huge cedar trunks in Whyte's life. This pastor's commentary on Bunyan's classic brims with acute intelligence and warm devotion. Whyte is a pastor directing pastors.

2. Richard Baxter, **THE REFORMED PASTOR**, edited by Hugh Martin (1956). Baxter paid more attention to his own life before God than he did to the spiritual conditions of his parishioners. Most of us reverse those proportions. But Baxter did it right — or, better, spent his years at Kidderminster trying to get it right.

3. Martin Thornton, **PASTORAL THEOLOGY: REORIENTATION** (1958). Thornton, an Anglican priest in England, is the sanest pastoral theologian of the century. He bypasses the fads and drives to the center where prayer shapes pastoral work "new every morning." I beat the drums for Thornton every chance I get. (He writes to a specifically Anglican context, but I find it easy to make compensating adjustments to my non-Anglican situation.)

4. Eduard Thurneysen, **A THEOLOGY OF PASTORAL CARE,** translated by Jack Worthington and Thomas Weiser (1962). Thurneysen the pastor and Barth the professor had a long, admiring, and interactive friendship. Thurneysen put Barth's thinking to the test in his pastoral practice; Barth put Thurneysen's experience into his dogmatics. They confirmed each other.

5. Frederick Buechner, **THE FINAL BEAST** (1965). When I became a pastor I supposed that the vocation would protect and nurture my spirituality — that since I was about the business of Scripture and prayer all day long, my whole Christian life would be easier. It didn't turn out that way. This novel is an account of how it did in fact turn out. The details and names in the story of this pastor are different, but the intricacies of temptation, the even greater intricacies of grace, and the infinite spiritualities of holiness are the same.

6. Wendell Berry, **THE UNSETTLING OF AMERICA** (1977). Berry is a Kentucky farmer who also writes novels, poems, and essays. Every time he writes "farm" I substitute "parish" or "congregation." It works every time. I have learned more usable pastoral theology from this farmer than from all my academic professors.

7. Benedict, **THE RULE** (collected in *Western Asceticism*, translated by Owen Chadwick, 1958). Not strictly for pastors, but Benedict was a pastor to monks, and his wisdom and counsel travel well through the centuries. He understood the nature of the spiritual life that was lived for others and in relation to others. For those of us who are responsible for shaping a spiritual community in our congregation, Benedict is a wise companion.

8. John Henry Newman, **GRAMMAR OF ASSENT** (1870). Pastors, it must never be forgotten, have *minds*. Newman's mind, some think the keenest of the last century, found its fullest flowering not in an academic but in a pastoral setting. No one exercised and practiced intelligence in the parish context better than Newman.

9. Francis Trochu, **THE CURE D'ARS**, translated by Dom Ernest Graf (1927). The unpretentious French priest Jean Vianney, of the last century (1786-1859), in simplicity and holiness fashioned a lifelong pastoral presence in his village. It remains one of the most powerful models for honest pastoral work that we have. In the Roman Church he is the patron saint of parish priests.

10. Jonathan Edwards, **A TREATISE CONCERNING RELIGIOUS AFFECTIONS** (1959). Everything Edwards wrote came out of his experience with his congregation. He was always trying to understand and protect, nurture and develop the juncture of divine revelation and human experience. What gets separated out so often as psychology on the one hand and theology on the other was joined and integrated in Edwards in the life of the pastor.

11. Dietrich Bonhoeffer, **SPIRITUAL CARE,** translated by Jay Rochelle (1985). This is one of the last of Bonhoeffer's books to be translated and confirms his primary genius as pastor and pastoral theologian.

12. Jean Leclercq, **THE LOVE OF LEARNING AND THE DESIRE FOR GOD** (1974). For a thousand years the monk was the primary spiritual guide in Europe. The accumulated experience of that millennium is one of the richest but most woefully neglected sources for pastoral work. Leclercq, a Benedictine in Luxembourg, knows this world better than anyone.

13. David Hansen, **THE ART OF PASTORING** (1994). Going against the stream of ecclesiastial technology and clerical professionalizing, Hansen presents the pastoral vocation as essentially an art — a weave of intuition and perception, of prayer and parable, of humility in the service of Jesus and unsentimental affection for sinners. This is not what most pastors aspire toward, but it is what most Christians wish their pastors would be.

14. Walter Wangerin, Jr., **THE ORPHEAN PASSAGES** (1985). In the large context of storytelling, Wangerin engages us in a conversation on pastoral theology: language, faith, suffering, Christ, death, resurrection, holiness, and stories — always stories. But this conversation all takes place in the context of the person who learns theology, develops in the faith, and experiences grace in the dailiness of pastoral preaching and visiting and sinning. A pastor is also a Christian — or can be, given extraordinary grace. A pastor is not a pew-Christian raised to the fifth power and so a pulpit Christian. Pastors live the identical details and dimensions of the faith that all Christians live, but the *setting* is different and the devil customizes his temptations to the circumstances, even as the Lord does his blessings. Wangerin embraces and understands these details better than anyone I know — he searches out the exact *feel*, the precise *texture* of the faith for the men and women who have "Reverend" or "Pastor" prefixed to their names.

15. Reinhold Niebuhr, **LEAVES FROM THE NOTEBOOKS OF A TAMED CYNIC** (1929). Niebuhr, who later in life became one of North America's finest theologians, began his work in the second decade of this century as a pastor of a blue-collar, working congregation in industrial Detroit. His thirteen years as a young pastor in difficult conditions, learning to preach Christ truly and serve people honestly, are chronicled in these pages. Even though the conditions in which I worked out my pastoral vocation were very different, the spirituality that was involved was nearly identical, and I delighted in having a companion in the work. This is not an expert telling us how to do our work from a position of authority, but a companion in making mistakes, experiencing failures, realizing the doggedness of the work and amazing grace.

XIII

Jesus

Jesus is the central figure in the spiritual life. His life is, precisely, *revelation*. He brings out into the open what we could never have figured out for ourselves, never guessed in a million years. He is God among us — speaking, acting, healing, helping. God in our language, in our history.

The four Gospel writers tell us everything we need to know about Jesus. We Christians read, ponder, study, believe, and pray these four Gospels, and find them a full and complete revelation of God's will and love for us.

But we also find the four Gospel writers quite spare and reticent in their accounts of the revelation. There is so much that they do *not* tell us. There is so much more we would like to know. Our imaginations itch to fill in the details. What did Jesus look like? How did he grow up? How did his childhood friends treat him? What did he do all those years in the carpentry shop?

And so, of course, there are always writers around to satisfy our curiosities — to tell us what Jesus was *really* like. But "lives" of Jesus — imaginative constructs of Jesus' life with all the childhood influences, emotional tones, neighborhood gossip, and so-cial/cultural/political dynamics worked in — are notoriously un-satisfactory. What we always seem to get is not the Jesus who reveals God to us, but a Jesus who develops some ideal or justifies some cause of the writer. When we finish the book we realize that we have less of Jesus, not more.

This itch to know more about Jesus than the canonical Gospel writers chose to tell us actually started early on in the second century. The first people who filled in the blanks in the story had wonderful imaginations but were somewhat deficient in veracity; they omitted to tell us that the supplementary details were the product of their imaginations. Some of them wrote under apostolic pseudonyms to provide authority to their inventions. Others claimed actual Holy Spirit inspiration for their fictions. It wasn't long before the church got more or less fed up with this imaginative tinkering and creative expansion with Jesus and said it had to stop. The church leaders rendered their decision: Mat-thew, Mark, Luke, and John are the last word on Jesus. There is nothing more to be said on the subject.

The ban on inventing new Jesus stories and sayings actually released the imagination for doing something that is proper to it — joining Mary in pondering Jesus in our hearts (Luke 2:19, 51), imagining our own selves into the presence of Jesus as presented by the Gospel writers, into the presence of God as revealed in Jesus; or imagining other settings in which Jesus is met and either crucified again or believed in again. And we have been doing it ever since in sermons and Bible studies, in stories and poems, in hymns and prayers.

1. Romano Guardini, **THE LORD** (1954). Guardini — im-mensely learned and widely experienced in the Christian way, writing books on many subjects, giving leadership to European Christians through many crises — comes to Jesus in the simplicity and trust of a child. He writes thoughtfully, believingly, and prayerfully as he works his leisurely way through all that the Gospel writers tell us that Jesus said and did.

2. David Smith, **THE DAYS OF HIS FLESH** (1905). A diligent, devout, and sober presentation of Jesus against the background of what we know of the social and economic, political and religious conditions of the first century. It gathers the best of nineteenth-century scholarship on Jesus and presents it coherently — so well, indeed, that it remains among us as a classic. Scholars have improved upon many of the historical details found here, but not in reverence and understanding of the person and ministry of Jesus.

3. Günther Bornkamm, **JESUS OF NAZARETH** (1960). Scholars do not always serve us well with their exegetical and historical scrutinies; rather than bringing Jesus into clearer focus, they often obscure him in a fog of minutiae. But Bornkamm, a German professor, serves us very well indeed. He sifts through a century of archaeological and textual studies and presents his findings with concise and refreshing clarity.

4. François Mauriac, **THE LIFE OF JESUS** (1937). Mauriac, a novelist, writes simply as a believing Christian, giving witness to God become man. He writes with chaste restraint, repressing any novelistic tendencies he might have to embellish, detracting from the divine revelation. But he also employs a novelist's skill with words so that Jesus' humanity in detail after detail is vivid and actual.

5. G. K. Chesterton, **THE EVERLASTING MAN** (1925). Chesterton, with his typical exuberance and wit and devastating polemic, rescues Jesus from both learned (so-called) dismissal and

pious ignorance. For the issue of Jesus is not simply Jesus —
humankind is at issue. The way we look upon and treat Jesus is
the way we come to look upon and treat each other. The integrity
of humanity is at stake in the divinity of Jesus. No one has exposed
these practical interdependencies better than Chesterton.

6. Malcolm Muggeridge, **JESUS REDISCOVERED**. Muggeridge
was a British journalist who lived most of his life on what we
think of as the front pages of the modern world, cynical and secular.
And then, late in life, he became a Christian. The unexpected and
total reversal of values and behavior and opinion provides a unique
perspective for reflecting on the uniqueness of Jesus.

7. Pär Lagerkvist, **BARABBAS** (1951). The life of Jesus shapes
our lives, whether we want it to or not. We cannot escape the
defining presence of Jesus. Barabbas, not a disciple, not a follower,
not a believer, was neverthless alive only because of Jesus and
never able to forget it. That, at least, is the way Lagerkvist, the
Nobel Prize-winning Norwegian novelist, imagines the story of
Barabbas. Because most of us know the story of Jesus so well, it
is hard not to lapse into clichés and stereotypes when telling it.
But by taking the indirect approach and seeing Jesus only in the
influence he has on Barabbas, every detail becomes fresh again.
There is not a cliché in the book.

8. Dorothy Sayers, **THE MAN BORN TO BE KING: A
Play-Cycle on the Life of our Lord and Saviour Jesus Christ**
(1943). When this drama was first aired on British radio during
World War II, proper churchgoers were scandalized to hear Jesus
talking in the accent and vocabulary common to the streets of
London. Shrill accusations of heresy disturbed the peace nearly
as much as the nightly raids from the Nazi Luftwaffe. There is
a certain strain of spirituality, and much too common, that has

far more difficulty in dealing with the humanity of Jesus than with his divinity.

9. Francis Thompson, **THE HOUND OF HEAVEN** (1923). The metaphors and rhythms of this long poem insinuate themselves into the imagination and continue to surprise, arrest, and confront us with the insistent *there*ness of Jesus. No one writes this kind of poetry today, nor should they, but its very unfashionableness reinforces, for me, its spiritual accuracy.

10. Alexander Whyte, **THE WALK, CONVERSATION, AND CHARACTER OF JESUS CHRIST OUR LORD** (1905). When all the studies are in, and all the books written and read, it turns out that the pulpit is still the best place from which to hear about Jesus. Jesus is not so much a subject to be studied as a person to be preached, and Whyte *preaches* Jesus. Oh, how he preaches Jesus.

11. P. T. Forsyth, **THE PERSON AND PLACE OF JESUS CHRIST** (1910). Is it possible to be theologically accurate without being pedantic? Is it possible to be theologically passionate without becoming soupy? The art of theology is on the one hand to avoid reducing Jesus to propositions and information, and on the other hand to present him as a compelling Lord and inviting Savior on his own terms. Forsyth is a theological artist who does this for us as well as anyone and better than most.

XIV

Mysteries

When my children were young, I was full of devout idealism regarding ways in which we as a family would replicate the church as we gathered around the dinner table. Especially on Sundays. When we returned home after a morning of worship and sat down to Sunday dinner, I would attempt to initiate and direct a discussion that would bring the prayer and praise from the sanctuary into the eating and drinking at our dining room table. I would ask what they thought of the second hymn, or how they liked the introduction to the sermon. Did they notice the novel twist the assisting elder had given to pronouncing Melchizedek in the Scripture reading? No real conversation ever developed. One Sunday in a moment of inspired desperation I took another tack. I said, "After the pastoral prayer, Mr. Green, head bowed, never straightened up. Those around him thought he was still praying. After the benediction when he still hadn't moved, he was discovered dead. Murdered. How was it done, and what was the motive?" Conversation developed. *Real* conversation. What it lacked in devoutness it made up for in liveliness. We searched the Scripture readings for clues, sifted the hymns for evidence, examined the possibilities of sin behind the congregational facade of Presbyterian rectitude. Each week there would be another victim.

Our cottage industry in murder mysteries didn't last long — a few weeks as I recall. But it was enough to introduce me to the escapist pleasures of detective fiction. I soon found that it is a pleasure much indulged in by scholars, pastors and theologians. Gabriel Marcel always insisted that we have to choose whether we will treat life as a problem to be solved or as a mystery to be entered. Why then do so many of the men and women who choose to enter the mystery slip aside from time to time to read mysteries that aren't mysteries at all, but problems that always get solved by the last page? I think one reason may be that right and wrong, so often obscured in the ambiguities of everyday living, are cleanly delineated in the murder mystery. The story gives us moral and intellectual breathing room when we are about to be suffocated in the hot air and heavy panting of relativism and subjectivism.

Pastors and priests, associated vocationally with a holy God, spend most of their time with sinners of every conceivable variety. Some of them are quite ready to confess their sins; but concealment is also practiced extensively. Because their life experiences immerse them in the vagaries of sin, men and women in holy orders are splendidly qualified for detecting it. For the most part I have limited myself in these annotations to murder mysteries that involve a religious figure — pastor, priest, monk, nun, rabbi — as a central figure in the plot.

1. G. K. Chesterton, **THE FATHER BROWN STORIES** (1929). The mild and soft-spoken Father Brown, unassuming and unobtrusive, always took people by surprise when he solved a crime. They didn't realize that a lifetime of hearing confessions was as good a training as one could ask for in crime detection. W. H. Auden, confessed Christian and self-confessed detective story addict, wrote, "Father Brown solved his cases, not by approaching them objectively like a scientist or a policeman, but by subjectively imagining himself to be the murderer, a process which is good not only for the murderer but for Father Brown himself because, as he said, 'it gives a man his remorse beforehand'" (*The Dyer's Hand* [New York: Random House, 1962], p. 156).

2. Ellis Peters, **THE PILGRIM OF HATE** (1984). The medieval monk Brother Cadfael, while solving murders, manages to dispense an immense amount of medicinal, psychological, and spiritual lore along the way. (There are at least twenty Cadfael mysteries now; and something like a cult forming around them.)

3. Virginia Stem Owens, **MULTITUDE OF SINS** (1994). It's not every day that I am entertained by a mystery novel and edified by a sermon at the same time. In the course of working through a tangle of crime, prison chaplain Kamowski lets loose with a sermon that is better than most that we hear from our pulpits. This is the third in a sequence of mystery novels (the first two are *Point Blank* [1991] and *Congregation* [1992]) set in a small Texas community where criminal acts evoke Christian insights.

4. William X. Kienzle, **THE ROSARY MURDERS** (1979). A serial murderer in Detroit gives Father Koesler something to do besides hearing confessions and conducting Mass. But sin and sanctity still frame the work. There are now upwards of sixteen Father Koesler stories.

5. Harry Kemelmen, **SUNDAY THE RABBI STAYED HOME** (1969). Besides solving murders, Rabbi David Small provides non-Jewish readers with a thorough orientation in what rabbis do and how a synagogue community operates. There are now rabbi stories for every day of the week.

6. D. M. Greenwood, **CLERICAL ERRORS** (1991). Theodora Braithwaite, a deaconess in the Anglican Church, has a sharp eye for detecting the sin that results in dead bodies and the sin that results in dead souls. Greenwood is equally good at plotting murders and discerning evil.

7. David Willis McCullough, **THINK ON DEATH** (1991). Ziza Todd, a red-headed Presbyterian seminarian on the threshold of ordination to the Gospel Ministry, discovers herself, without having registered or paid tuition fees, enrolled in a graduate course in sin, chicanery, and murder. There are astute observations throughout on the propensity of utopian spirituality to breed its own species of sin.

8. Rex Stout, **FER-DE-LANCE** (1934). Nero Wolfe, the fat detective featured in the numerous Rex Stout murder mysteries, is not a clergyman, but for thirty years I have amused myself and some of my friends by reading him as a parable of the Christian contemplative presence in the world. The popular imagination, dulled by contemporaneity, sees nothing in the Nero Wolfe stories but detection. But Stout has written a body of work every bit as theologically perspicuous as Swift with the result that he hits the best-seller lists as a clever and resourceful detective novelist. To his financial benefit, of course, but still, for a serious writer to be misunderstood so completely must be humiliating no matter what the bank balance. But once the theological intent is suggested, the barest sleuthing quickly discerns Nero Wolfe as a type of the church's presence in the world. The most evident thing about him, his body, provides an analogue to the Church. His vast bulk is evidence of his "weight," recalling the etymology of the biblical "glory." More than anything else he is there, visibly. He must be reckoned with. He is corpulent or nothing. And the Church is the body of Christ. Along with an insistence on bodily presence

there is a corresponding observation that there is nothing attractive about that body. His body is subject to calumny and jokes.
His genius is in his mind and his style. He does not fawn before
customers, nor seek "contacts" (a word, incidentally, that he
would never use. He once was found ripping apart a dictionary,
page by page, and burning it because it legitimized "contact" as a
transitive verb). Wolfe will not leave his house on business, that
is, accommodate himself to the world's needs. He is a center
around which the action revolves, a center of will and meditation,
not a center of power or activity. He provides a paradigm for
Christian spirituality that, while reticent and reserved, is there in
vast presence when needed. He has no need for advertising techniques or public relations programs. He is there and needed because there is something wrong in the world (murder and other
criminal extremes). He models a contemplative life which is not
here to be loved, not designed to inspire affection. It is massive,
central, important — a genius, in fact. But you don't have to like
it. In all this there is an implied criticism of a Church that has
succumbed to public relations agents who have mounted Christian pulpits to make the church attractive — to personalize her,
to sentimentalize her. Wolfe, as Christian ministry, levels a rebuke
against that kind of thing. It follows that there is disdain for
defensive explanations — a Barthian avoidance of "apologetics"
to a world that seeks assurance of its reliability and effectiveness.
To that kind of inquiry he says: "I can give you my word, but I
know what it's worth and you don't." The spiritual life is cheap-
ened when it tries to defend itself or make itself acceptable in
terms the world can understand.

9. Ronald Knox, **THE FOOTSTEPS AT THE LOCK** (1928).
Strictly speaking, this one doesn't fit into my guidelines — but it
was *written* by a priest. And written so well that I couldn't bear
to leave it out. Knox was one of the best practitioners of English

prose of the century, writing with an easy elegance that rivals the ingenuity of his plotting. When he wasn't writing murder mysteries he led retreats and gave us a modern translation of the Holy Scriptures from the Latin.

10. Ralph McInerny, **JUDAS PRIEST** (1991). Father Dowling is good at solving murders; he is equally good at seeing through the lies of contemporary culture and exposing the empty-headed, soul-draining living that parades itself as modern and enlightened.

11. Margeret Frazer, **THE NOVICE'S TALE** (1992). A medieval monastery in England is the setting. Nuns implement the action. Pre-Reformation spirituality provides atmosphere and background.

12. Erik Routley, **THE PURITAN PLEASURE OF THE DETECTIVE STORY.** This Scots pastor legitimized the reading of detective stories for all of us who feel guilty when caught doing it. Assembling the names of famous scholars, pastors, and theologians who took delight in reading about other people's sins, Routley reflects on the underlying spiritual motives that contribute to the pleasure.

13. Umberto Eco, **THE NAME OF THE ROSE** (1983). Set in a fourteenth-century Franciscan monastery in Italy where multiple murders are occurring, Brother William, a disciple of Roger Bacon, trained by his master in the inductive reasoning that equipped the European intellect to inaugurate the age of science, is here put to the fictional task of solving murders. We are not only entertained by the sleuthing of Brother William, but immensely instructed in the actual historical conditions in which the fresh innocence of Franciscan spirituality rapidly decomposed into a proliferation of religious heresies that turned Italy for a time into a spiritual garbage dump.

XV

Commentaries

The first Bible that I chose for myself was a Scofield Reference Bible, purchased with my own money when I was thirteen years old. It was bound in Morocco leather and printed on fine India paper. It cost $10.95, a healthy sum in 1946. I had determined to get it when I heard an adult whom I respected say that this particular Bible was indispensable for understanding Scripture. My first chosen Bible was also my first commentary on the Bible.

Ten years later I rejected, with more vehemence than was probably necessary, nearly everything that Scofield had written in his notes on the scriptural text. I resented the intrusion of his headings and outlines. But however thoroughly I came to quarrel with the man, I do not quarrel with his gift to me of a lifelong love of commentaries.

I read commentaries the way some people read novels, from beginning to end, skipping nothing. I admit that they are weak in plot and character development, but their devout attention to words and syntax keeps me turning the pages. Plot and character

— the plot of salvation, the character of Messiah — are everywhere implicit in a commentary and persistently assert their presence even when unmentioned through scores, even hundreds, of pages. The power of these ancient nouns and verbs century after century to call forth intelligent discourse from learned men and women continues to be a staggering wonder to me.

Among those for whom Scripture is a passion, reading commentaries has always seemed to me analogous to the gathering of football fans in the local bar, replaying in endless detail the game they have just watched, arguing (maybe even fighting) over observations and opinion, and lacing the discourse with gossip about the players. The level of knowledge evident in these boozy colloquies is impressive. These fans have watched the game for years; the players are household names to them; they know the fine print in the rulebook and pick up every nuance on the field. And they care immensely about what happens in the game. Their seemingly endless commentary is evidence of how much they care. Like them, I relish in a commentary not bare information but conversation with knowledgeable and experienced friends, probing, observing, questioning the biblical text. Absorbed by this plot that stretches grandly from Genesis to Revelation, captured by the messianic presence that in death and resurrection saves us one and all, there is much to notice, much to talk over.

1. George Adam Smith, **ISAIAH**, 2 volumes (1889). George Adam Smith was pastor of Queen's Cross Free Church in Aberdeen (Scotland) when he wrote his *Isaiah*. While there, he integrated a powerful preaching ministry with pastoral work and academic pioneering. These were the days of the new criticism in biblical studies that regularly polarized the church into an obscurantist pietism on the one hand, and an arrogant intellectualism on the other. But Smith demonstrated that polarization was not inevitable. In that context, this commentary is a brilliant

achievement, fiercely honest intellectually, and passionately evangelical spiritually.

2. William Temple, **READINGS IN ST. JOHN'S GOSPEL**
(1959). As a bishop in the Church of England, William Temple
took his diocesan clergy on retreat once a year and nurtured them
with readings and commentary from John's Gospel. Temple was
a fine theologian and a true pastor; this book exhibits the accurate
integration of learning and praying that took place in his life.
Informality, simplicity, and profundity all come together here.

3. Gerhard von Rad, **GENESIS**, translated by John Marks
(1961). I met Gerhard von Rad only once, and that briefly. I was
a guest at "The Symposium," a book club in Princeton that con-
ducted a monthly dinner meeting at the old Princeton Inn. That
evening, von Rad, on a visit from Germany, was also a guest,
invited by his longtime friend, Professor Otto Piper. Piper introduced von Rad and asked him to say a few words. The room was
dimly lit, and I was about thirty feet away. He stood and spoke. I
remember him as tall and craggy, an alpine figure. He talked for
probably no more than two or three minutes, but the impression
on me was powerful. There was no small talk, none of the pleas-
antries one comes to expect on such occasions. Without preamble,
he started talking about Abraham. I don't recall the content of
his remarks but remember the repetition of "mystery," "darkness,"
"faith," and "prayer." As von Rad spoke from a shadowed part of
that room, for a few moments Abraham was present for me in his
person, a real presence out of the centuries, out of the shadows,
the vibrations of faith, and the energies of prayer. Years earlier in
seminary, my Hebrew professor had told me that German was the
most important Semitic language, so I set out to learn it. Von
Rad's *Der Heilige Krieg im alten Israel* was the first book that I read
all the way through in German. In the process, Hebrew and

German became fused for me in the person of von Rad. Now, looking at him and listening to him, all the complexities and difficulties of the two languages distilled into something distinctly spiritual, something Abrahamic, something mystic. When I arrived home after the Princeton meeting, the first thing I did was purchase von Rad's commentary on Genesis. On page after page I found confirmation of my first impressions of the commentator: strong, spare, ascetic, mystic. In and behind the sinewy scholarship, I was conscious of urgency and faith. Lives were at stake here. Every sentence counted. Theology was wedded to philology. I learned later that the commentary had gotten its start many years earlier in 1944 when he expounded the book of Genesis daily to his fellow inmates at a prisoner of war camp in Bad Kreusnach. This was a book authenticated in adversity and pastoral care.

4. Austin Farrer, **THE REVELATION** (1964). I grew up in a church that read and interpreted Scripture with imagination. Learning was not greatly prized but imagination was given free rein. Education was, in fact, suspect, a compensation, I was told, for failure to believe in the power of God to be "his own interpreter" through the immediate outpouring of the Holy Spirit. But the telling of stories, the invention of allegories, the uncovering of the "deeper meanings" — these were held in high repute. When I, not heeding the warnings of my pious friends, went far away to be schooled in theology and the Scriptures, these valuations were reversed. Imagination was treated condescendingly; the rational and critical intelligence was honored. Unthinkingly, I accepted the thinking of my teachers. By the time I learned of the hermeneutic polarization in the early church between Antioch and Alexandria, I was firmly in the Antiochene camp, heaping abuse on the Alexandrines. The Antioch interpreters were sober, historically grounded, as meticulous with the text as a watchmaker. The Alexandria interpreters were wildly extravagant, bounding off the text like a gymnast off a trampoline. I was being carefully trained in criticism and grammar, learning to be responsible and rational before the biblical text. My position was confirmed by what I learned in church history as I discovered the havoc wrought among the faithful through the centuries by preachers and teachers whose feverish zeal used the Bible, as Ellen Goodman once said, as if it were a Rorschach test rather than a religious test, reading more into the ink than they read out of it. And then I came across the work of Austin Farrer and realized that there was still a case to be made for Alexandria. Imagination cannot be banished from the hermeneutical task. Poetry is a biblical mode. Story is a gospel genre. Farrer, Warden of Keble College, Oxford, and a scholar in New Testament and philosophy, was a disciplined thinker and knowledgeable exegete who was at the same time extravagantly imaginative. As I read Farrer on the Gospels and the Apocalypse, I found myself at home again in the colorful world of my childhood and youth, playful in the analogical, delighting in the anagogical, but with one large difference — this was an imagination informed by and submissively disciplined to every grammatical insight and historical datum available. In his commentary on the Revelation (1964), Farrer is at his best, wonderfully showing the "right brain" and "left brain" together in courteous discourse, the fierce Antiochene wolf and the playful Alexandrine lamb lying down in peace on the holy mountain.

5. Gordon Fee, **1 CORINTHIANS** (1987). Textual criticism, the scrupulous study and exacting judgments that go into establishing the most accurate text possible for our Greek and Hebrew Scriptures, is sometimes supposed to be least "spiritual" of all scholarly pursuits, grimly stereotyped in Robert Browning's Grammarian, ". . . in love with *hoti*, dead from the waist down." The work is, after all, mostly a matter of collecting and arranging thousands of small bits of data — counting words and variants of words. But the stereotypical supposition shatters on the pages of this commentary. Whenever Professor Fee, eminent among the church's textual critics, touches on a text-critical or exegetical matter, it characteristically springs to life — we see that words matter immensely, and why; it is impossible to give too much care to the minute and precise details of this biblical text. But there is far more here than an accumulation of precise notations; there is a passionate and wise entering into the life of the Spirit that created the Corinthian church and occasioned this letter. And this combination — exegetical precision and passionate spirituality — is rare indeed. The Corinthian letter, when read carelessly or ideologically, has caused much mischief in the church, splitting Christians into factions, exacerbating controversy. But under Professor Fee's disciplined intelligence and exuberant spirit, the text comes into its own as God's Word shaping a Christian life of wise and robust maturity.

6. F. Dale Bruner, **THE CHRISTBOOK** (1987) and **THE CHURCHBOOK** (1990). This is the kind of commentary I most want: a *theological* wrestling with Scripture. Bruner grapples with the text, not only as a technical exegete (although he also does that very well) but as a church theologian, caring passionately about what these words tell us about God and ourselves. Here he places his considerable teaching gifts at the service of the Christian community, caring as much about us as he cares about the text. His Matthew commentary is in the grand traditions of Augustine, Calvin, and Luther — expansive and leisurely, loving the text, the people in it, and the Christians who read it.

7. Gregory of Nyssa, **THE SONG OF SONGS**, translated and edited by Herbert Musurillo, S.J., in *From Glory to Glory* (1961). The Song of Songs may be the most commented upon book in

our Scriptures, despite the omission of the name of God in its
pages. The subject is love. Both Jews and Christians have found
this text endlessly fascinating, inviting, and nurturing. The rationalist critics of our day tend to be condescending and dismissive
of the Song, reducing it to "nothing but" a collection of erotic
verse. But devout readers find that these love poems still reflect
and refract the insights and truths, the beauties and pains of love
in all its many forms, variations, and combinations: love between
the sexes, God's love for us and our love for God, Christ's love
for the Church and the Church's love for Christ. Of all the
excellent commentators on this text, Gregory of Nyssa holds my
allegiance. Gregory, a fourth-century scholar and pastor, seems to
be present to the entire canon of Holy Scripture at once; he
constantly surprises and delights me as he shows me correspon-
dences, resonances, and relationships. He doesn't dissect Scripture
into bits and pieces; by reverently attending to the organic aliveness of each Spirit-connected word and sentence, he makes ex-
plicit what is everywhere implicit: these Scriptures are one Book
with one Author. He is at his best in the *Song of Songs*.

8. Brevard Childs, **EXODUS** (1974). The scholarship invested
in the Christian Scriptures in this twentieth century is quite
without precedent. No other century has had so many men and
women, equipped with so much learning and assisted with so
much technology, spend their lives studying and writing about the
Bible. We welcome this initially as a great boon; but very soon
we find ourselves buried under an avalanche of periodicals and
books, numbed by knowledge. We need someone to dig us out
and show us how to find our way through the knowledge without
being crushed by it. Brevard Childs of Yale Divinity School has
rescued many of us. He seems to be acquainted with everything
that is in the libraries in addition to keeping up with his significant

contemporaries. But Childs does more — he has formulated a method (canonical criticism) for holding it all together coherently so that the biblical story is kept intact. In the deluge of scholarly studies, he keeps our heads above water so that we can maintain our bearings and see where the gospel is leading us. His Exodus commentary is typical of his clarifying methodology and wise exegetical/theological judgments.

9. Charles Gore, **EPISTLE TO THE EPHESIANS** (1897). This letter is a primary text for the formation of mature Christian character and requires a mature Christian to comment on it. Lacking sanctity, a writer is in danger of trivializing or obscuring this extravagant exercise in Christian thinking and praying. Gore, a bishop in the Church of England a hundred years ago, qualifies in both intellect and spirit. The *way* he comments on Paul's theological poetry shows him to be of the same mind as the Spirit who inspired its writing in the first place.

10. F. Godet, **A COMMENTARY ON THE GOSPEL OF ST. LUKE**, translated by E. W. Shalders, 2 volumes (1870). There is a leisurely quality to this work that invites contemplative reflection, just as the Gospel itself does. Godet, a French professor, wrote this at a time when many scholars were intent on weeding everything out of the Scriptures that they couldn't explain or account for by a rigorous historical-critical methodology. They thought we modern men and women needed a Bible without mystery or miracle — indeed, without God. The atmosphere became tense and polemical. Voices became shrill. But not Godet; he never raised his voice; he never wrote a discourteous sentence. He consistently dealt gently and firmly with matters of controversy, but he did not write primarily to contest rationalist critics; his purpose was to affirm believing Christians. He wrote in the service of Luke and his Lord the Spirit.

11. Karl Barth, **THE EPISTLE TO THE PHILIPPIANS,** translated by James W. Leitch from the 1947 German edition (1962). Barth, best known as a theologian, was also a master of biblical exegesis; but most of his exegetical work is in the fine print of his multivolumed *Church Dogmatics*. But here, in his commentary on Philippians, the theological exegesis stands on its own — terse, accurate, targeted.

12. Brooke Foss Westcott, **THE EPISTLE TO THE HEBREWS** (1903). Westcott was one of the magisterial commentators of the nineteenth century. Besides collaborating (with Hort) on a landmark critical Greek text, he commented on several New Testament books. In *The Epistle to the Hebrews* he is at his characteristic best, weaving sharply observed philology with a deeply lived spirituality.

13. Martin Luther, **LECTURES ON ROMANS**, translated and edited by Wilhelm Pauck (1961). The great attraction of this commentary for me is that in addition to being a commentary on a pivotal piece of Scripture, it exhibits the working of a great mind and spirit as the Spirit is preparing him for the reformation of Christ's Church. Luther wrote this while he was still a monk, but most of the hermeneutical, theological, and ecclesiastical details that proved to be formative in the Reformation are on display in these pages. This is quintessential Luther: bombastic, personal, devout, and insightful.

XVI

Place

The work of salvation is always local. We regularly pray, ". . . on *earth* as it is in heaven." Geography is as essential to spirituality as theology. The creation of land and water, star and planet, tree and mountain, grass and flower provides ground and environment for the blessings of providence and the mysteries of salvation. But in a world that is obsessively converting all landscape into real estate, it is easy to miss this.

The covenant always has the creation for its context. Nothing spiritual in our Scriptures is served apart from the material. Creation, Incarnation, Sacraments, all these are integral to the gospel. When God fashioned a universal gospel for "all the world," he became incarnate on a few square miles of Palestinian hills and valleys. An accurate street address is far more important in the proclamation of the gospel than a world map. Words like Nazareth, Shiloh, and Hebron appear on the same page as forgiveness, grace, and love.

But world conditions are not congenial to this honoring of locale. Ordinary place, the place of residence and work, is dismissed with terms such as "backwater," "hick town," "out-of-the-way," "regional," "provincial," "the sticks." Places that are honored are places to visit such as Bermuda or places to be entertained such as Disney World. Exotic scenery and exciting diversion give value to place, but place as such is limitation and confinement, a place to be stuck. So successful is the devil in convincing us that God's creation is a millstone on the neck of our spirituality that we resort to the most unlikely expedients to confer value on our place: a house containing the bed George Washington slept in; a battle fought two hundred years ago, the victorious reign of a football team. When world conditions so debase our imaginations into a devaluation of place, we no longer have a context for faith in Jesus Christ. Faith is reserved for the far-off exotic, or faith is confined to the occasional ecstasy. It would never occur to us that the actual place in which we live and labor is adequate to support large spiritual enterprises like salvation and sanctification.

And so it is necessary that a love of locale be recovered: this street, these trees, this humidity, these houses. Without reverence for the local, obedience floats on the clouds of abstraction. Every time a rock is named, a flower identified, a house number located, a street walked, the gospel is served. By observing texture and color, by insisting on immediate particularity, space is cleared and location provided for yet another spin-off of the Incarnation, most of which came to its definitive form in small towns and down country roads.

1. George Adam Smith, **GEOGRAPHY OF THE HOLY LAND** (1894). Numerous atlases and geographies, with much improved topography, geology, and cartography of the Holy Land, have been published since this one (in 1894), but none rival this quite incredible immersion in the landscape, history, and spirituality of the land that cradled the revelation of God in Israel and Jesus. I have always felt

that given a choice between a week on tour in the Holy Land and a week alone with this book, a Christian would be a fool not to choose the book.

2. Egeria, **DIARY OF A PILGRIMAGE**, translated and annotated by George E. Gingras (1970). Pilgrimage has been virtually replaced, in our century, by tourism. Thousands of people annually make trips to the Holy Land and then put themselves under the ministrations of a tour guide who points out important sites, arranges for photographic opportunities, and spins sentimental anecdotes of doubtful authenticity. So it is wonderful to have access to a true pilgrim, and one of the first. Tourists go to see and take pictures; pilgrims go to pray and worship. Egeria, a Spanish woman (possibly a nun), spent three years living in Jerusalem and traveling in the Near East in the late fourth century.

3. Wendell Berry, **HARLAN HUBBARD, LIFE AND WORK** (1990). Rescued from obscurity by Wendell Berry, Hubbard's life is a powerful confirmation of the power of place, when accepted and loved and embraced, to form and inform a spirituality of simplicity, honesty, fidelity, and reverence. Berry's verdict on Hubbard: "His great legacy to us is the record of a long life fulfilled in the terms and conditions of the river valley in which it was mostly lived. It was not a life that ever assumed that it could be improved by mobility, either upward or lateral."

4. Belden C. Lane, **LANDSCAPES OF THE SACRED: Geography and Narrative in American Spirituality** (1988). This extended and thoughtful examination of the many and various ways that space and sanctity have interpenetrated each other on the North American continent provides detailed documentation of what most of us know in part: that the Holy Land is not the only holy land.

5. Kathleen Norris, **DAKOTA: A Spiritual Geography** (1993). A poet and sometimes lay preacher discovers and nurtures classic "desert spirituality" in a kind of antiphonal conversation between a rural Presbyterian congregation and a Benedictine monastery. Surprisingly (or maybe not!) the wisdom shaped in the deserts of Syria and Egypt is echoed and confirmed in motels and Jeeps on the plains of South Dakota.

6. John Muir, **JOURNALS**, from *The Wilderness World of John Muir*, edited by Edwin Way Teale (1954). John Muir tramped the continent, from Wisconsin to the Gulf and from the Sierras to Alaska. Everything he saw and heard and tasted and touched, he loved — and praised. In his extensive journals, he served as the secretary of creation's praise. Muir brought all the rigor and intensity of his Scotch Presbyterian upbringing to the contemplation of God's creation. No Calvinist theologian was more meticulous with the doctrines of salvation and sanctification than Muir was with the revelations of God that he received in Douglas firs and calving glaciers.

7. Barry Lopez, **ARCTIC DREAMS** (1986). The polar extremes of our planet seem to bring the best out of those who enter them. So much *absence* gives room for uncluttered experiences of *presence*. And, of course, nothing remotely lukewarm can exist there. The Arctic is a cathedral sanctuary for Lopez. He enters it with awe; his writing whispers his reverence.

8. Paul Tournier, **A PLACE OF YOUR OWN** (1968). This Swiss physician was one of the truly wise Christians of our century. He understood the human soul accurately, with immense compassion, and always in hope. In this work he establishes the spiritual significance of place for a people who characteristically hurry from one place to another, who live their lives *dis*placed.

9. Norman MacLean, **A RIVER RUNS THROUGH IT AND OTHER STORIES** (1976). I know a man who used to buy this book in lots of ten or twenty and give it away, as he put, to "those who are worthy of reading it." He gave me a copy. It soon became a family book, as my wife and children and I would read it aloud to each other. One reason that we liked it so much was that it gave dignity and a sense of holiness to *our* place, a place that was home to us. The story MacLean writes takes place a hundred miles from where I grew up in Montana and where our family returned each summer for holiday. We already knew it was a holy place, but the book confirmed and deepened our reverence. The book functioned as a shrine, calling attention to *this* place: *this* is holy ground — worship God *here*.

10. Francis of Assisi, **THE LITTLE FLOWERS** (c. 1330). These stories and memories of Francis were collected and written down a hundred years or so after his death. They show Francis as perhaps our finest witness to the spirituality of place. He is certainly our most exuberant. But place for Francis didn't at all mean beautiful scenery, it meant the stuff of creation by and in which he served God, and much of it in ruin. He repaired churches, kissed the sores of lepers, and felt and exhibited in his own body the place of Christ's wounds. On a few square miles of hilly *place* in central Italy, he walked and prayed, sang and suffered, preached and fasted the Holy Gospel with his feet always on Holy Ground.

XVII

Saints

Hagiography, writing about holy men and women, is a no-toriously failed genre. It gets high marks in boredom and dishonesty, and not much else. I very much doubt whether Foxe's *Book of Martyrs*, the staple hagiography of my childhood, did much to further holy living in me or my friends. Mostly, as I remember, it replaced fear of God with the fear of Catholics. And Butler's *Lives of the Saints*, a work of unquestionable usefulness, is as often used, by scholars at least, to debunk sanctity as to confirm it.

All of us have impulses from time to time to live a holy life — life lived as it should be, life true and good and beautiful, life lived for and in and by means of our Creator, Redeemer, and Sanctifier. And then someone telephones with an invitation to the hockey game, or we notice that the salad needs oregano, or the crabgrass in the lawn suddenly becomes a pressing priority. We are distracted by the mundane and forfeit, for yet another time, the holy. Or so we assume.

And then we find ourselves in the company of a writer or writers who penetrate the surface pieties and show us what the holy life is really like, that it is the hockey game and the oregano and the crabgrass that provide the raw material for holiness. Holiness is not being nice. A holy life isn't a matter of men and women being polite with God, but of humans who accept and enter into God's work of shaping salvation out of the unlikely materials of our sin and ignorance, our ambition and waywardness — also our loves and aspirations and nobilities — but never by smoothing over our rough edges. Holiness is not polish.

All Christians, in some way or another, are about the business of holy living, whether we have acquired a suitable vocabulary for it or not. But it is difficult to know exactly what it consists of. We hardly know what to look for anymore. For the last hundred years and more, those who have set themselves up as our authorities in how to live have been taking us on thrilling roller-coaster prospects of either social utopianism or psychological fulfillment — or both. And we are worse. The only things that have improved, if that is the word for it, are our capacities to move faster and spend more.

Herman Melville once wrote to a friend, "I love all men who *dive*." Most of us do. But where do we find them? Not in the men and women who attract attention. The trivial and evil feed the appetite for gossip in a journalistic culture. Neither goodness nor righteousness makes headlines. Anything that cannot be programmed for mass production, particularly moral excellence, is discarded. Maturity, since it cannot be mastered in a semester course, is no longer a personal goal.

Our ancestors were wiser. They looked around for saints, looked for the men and women whose lives were courageously conversant with God, and let them be their teachers in how to live as human beings, which is to say, how to live holy lives. Our secularized world, surfeited on celebrities and victims, has lost the capacity to see God working in ordinary and often unlikely people, that is, to recognize saints. The word itself has been so drained of meaning that it is more likely to be heard as a disclaimer — "I'm no saint" — than as an honorific. Leon Bloy puts us on the way to recovering appreciation and insight in his blunt and bold sentence, "The only sadness, not to be a saint" (Tristesse — de pas etre Saint).

1. Jacobus de Voragine, **THE GOLDEN LEGEND**, translated by William Caxton (1485). This is the most influential of the medieval gatherings of the stories of the saints, arranged according to the sequence in which they are remembered through the church year.

2. G. K. Chesterton, **ST. THOMAS AQUINAS** (1923) and **ST. FRANCIS OF ASSISI** (1933). Chesterton admires without idolizing; he celebrates without trivializing; he understands without patronizing. He shows us these two extravagantly different saints not in contradiction but as paradox: Thomas, mostly mind and intelligence; Francis, mostly body and intuition. But equally saints, the one exhibiting sanctity in serious thinking, the other in playful poverty. These are my favorite saint books.

3. Phyllis McGinley, **SAINT-WATCHING** (1969). Saints are human. Sanctity does not elevate us above our common humanity, but immerses us more deeply in it. The more sanctity, the more humanity. McGinley, a poet of humorous light verse, pulls the saints off the pedestals on which they have been ignorantly placed, and introduces us to men and women who share all the quirks and oddities of the rest of us. Sometimes these oddities are funny, but McGinley never uses her humor to denigrate, only to humanize.

4. Frederick Buechner, **GODRIC** (1980) and **BRENDAN** (1987). In an age when most writers, it seems, are trying to show how evil or trivial or boring men and women can be, Buechner has taken on the task of rendering the ancient and holy human capacity for becoming a saint and showing us how it works. Everyone knows that we can, and often do, live badly. Not everyone knows that we can live holy. Buechner makes an end run around the formidable stereotype that blocks our imaginations, the idea that "sainthood is something people achieve, that you get to be holy more or less the way you get to be an Eagle Scout" and shows us the real thing. "Only saints," he says, "really interest me as a writer. There is so much life in them. They are so in touch with, so transparent to, the mystery of things that you never know what to expect from them." These novels present the holy life as exuberant, unpredictable, and earthy. Holiness, as Buechner presents it, is not a matter of cautiously avoiding moral mud puddles; it's something more like turning cartwheels in the Spirit.

5. Elie Wiesel, **SOULS ON FIRE** (1972). Incarcerated as a young person in the Auschwitz death camp, Wiesel was one of the few to come out of it alive. That early experience of being surrounded by evil and immersed in death was turned somehow into an adult vocation as a writer exulting in holiness and celebrating life. In addition to writing novels, Weisel does this by telling the stories of the Baal Shem Tov and his successors. The Baal Shem, an obscure Jew who lived in eighteenth-century Eastern Europe, ignited a revival of spirituality that spread wildly from community to community with a sense of playful wonder, readiness for miracle, and holy aliveness among poor, persecuted, and marginalized Jews. Hasidism, it was called, an exuberant explosion of stories and songs. Elie Wiesel tells the stories. This is the first of several similar books giving witness to the alive mysteries of holy lives.

6. René Fülöp-Miller, **THE SAINTS THAT MOVED THE WORLD** (1945). Five saints — Anthony, Augustine, Francis,

Ignatius, and Theresa — are selected and held up for admiration and, yes, emulation. This is a major attempt to incite a taste and appetite for the sanity and exuberance and wisdom of holy lives well lived for a world that is living very badly on secular junk food.

7. J. I. Packer, **QUEST FOR GODLINESS** (1990). The Puritans characteristically pursued a holy life with uncommon sanity and vigor. But for many in the modern world these attractive and exemplary lives have been obscured by distorting stereotypes. Instead of exciting our admiration, the term "puritan" is more likely to elicit aversion. Packer rescues the Puritans from ill-deserved dismissal, bringing them out into the clear light of day where we can see them for what they truly are — at the crest of imitable Christian spirituality.

8. Peter Brown, **AUGUSTINE OF HIPPO** (1967). Augustine's influence on the life of Christians is mostly healthy, but not entirely so. Because it is so many-dimensional and pervasive, it requires repeated consideration. We keep going back to this life again and again in trying to appreciate and understand the complex interconnections between personal experience and secular culture. Every visit with Augustine has its payoff — insight, warning, delight, vision, caution, desire. The Christian life is a large life, and Augustine lived it largely. Brown's biography does justice to both the tangled intricacies of the times and the profound simplicity that gradually came into being in this holy life.

9. W. E. Sangster, **THE PURE IN HEART** (1954). This wide-ranging, generous appreciation of saints, attempts (with marvelous success, I think) to convince Protestants that we ought to take the whole saint business much more seriously than has been our wont, and cultivate an appreciation for the men and women who call our attention to sanctity. Sangster, a British Methodist bishop, brings the Wesleyan concern for holiness into conjunction with Roman Catholic practice of veneration, and sets the two elements solidly in Holy Scripture.

11. Sigrid Undset, **SAGA OF SAINTS** (1934), **STAGES ON THE ROAD** (1934), **CATHERINE OF SIENA** (1954). After winning the world's attention with her immense novels of medieval Norway and receiving the Nobel Prize for them, Undset began writing biographies of saints, which have been pretty well ignored by the world. She wrote, "By degrees my knowledge of history convinced me that the only thoroughly sane people, of our civilization at least, seemed to be those queer men and women which the Catholic Church calls the Saints. . . . They seemed to know the true explanation of man's undying hunger for happiness."

12. Thérèse of Lisieux, **THE STORY OF A SOUL**, translated by Ronald Knox (1958). There is almost nothing to this woman — she did nothing that this world holds significant, knew no one important. She lived in obscurity, and for not very long (she died at the age of 24). It is, however, this pure simplicity, this childlike singularity, that commends her to us. "I tried my best," she wrote, "to do good on a small scale, having no opportunity to do it on a large scale."

13. Hans Urs von Balthasar, **THÉRÈSE OF LISIEUX** (1953). The purpose of this book is to rejuvenate theology, and the whole of Christian life, with a blood transfusion from a holy life. This simplist of holy lives is here honored by detailed, theological attention from one of our most complex minds.

14. David Farmer, **THE OXFORD DICTIONARY OF SAINTS** (1978). The vast field of hagiography is sorted through and pared down to something manageable with these judicious selections.

XVIII

Sin and the Devil

Martin Luther's test for spiritual leaders was, "What do they know of death and the devil?" I've amended it to "sin and the devil." Spirituality is far more than aspiration after good, after God. Our noblest intentions are susceptible to perversion and ruination. The first sin was committed in the best of all places by pure and innocent people. And so spirituality requires vigilance and discernment.

In fact, the more we hunger and thirst after God the more careful we need to be. Temptations to sin increase in subtlety as we develop in righteousness. We cannot afford to be naive in these matters.

The most popular contemporary spiritualities, though, pretty much ignore sin and the devil. The prevailing assumption seems to be that men and women are basically innocent and good, and all that is needed is training and encouragement to "become our best selves," and "blossom where we're planted." "Selfism" is fobbed off as spirituality. Sappy aphorisms from Kalil Gibran substitute for the tempered steel imperatives of Jesus.

But we Christians are well warned not to be fooled by superficial appearances of holiness, especially at those times when we think we catch glimpses of them in the mirror. We need rigorous and detailed schooling in the nuances of temptation, the ways of the devil, and our seemingly endless capacity for deceiving ourselves and being deceived. John of the Cross and Ignatius Loyola are our classic masters in the necessity and art of discernment, but we have many other wise guides in these matters and we do well to heed them.

1. C. S. Lewis, **THE SCREWTAPE LETTERS** (1944). Not often do we find a writer who has so much fun with something so serious. For Lewis does take the devil with dead seriousness. He believes, along with most of Christendom, that we who embrace the way of Christ are subject to seductions, lies, illusions, and other assorted and subtle deceits. But he also takes the position, along with our wisest ancestors, that the one thing the devil cannot stand is to be mocked. "The best way to drive out the devil, if he will not yield to texts of Scripture, is to jeer and flout him, for he cannot bear scorn," Martin Luther observed. I count this small book (thirty-one brief chapters) as one of the basic books of our century.

2. Denis de Rougement, **THE DEVIL'S SHARE** (1944). The premise of this book is that the devil's greatest achievement is to convince us that he doesn't exist. Or that he exists in some cartoon form that we don't have to take seriously in our common lives.

3. Søren Kierkegaard, **FEAR AND TREMBLING** (1844) and **THE SICKNESS UNTO DEATH** (1848). The testing/temptation of Abraham is a classic text for developing a mature discernment in matters of faith. In *Fear and Trembling* Kierkegaard looks at that story from every angle, turns it inside and out, and in so

99

doing disciplines our submission to this text. His intensity and seriousness are wonderful antidotes to the cheery bromides that we are so often subjected to. He returns to the theme, one of his "repetitions," in *Sickness unto Death,* and deepens his meditative penetration into the nature of sin, especially the fatal sin, despair.

4. Ernest Becker, **ESCAPE FROM EVIL** (1975). An assessment of evil more or less from the "outside" — for Becker does not embrace the Christian faith. In observing and studying the human condition, he arrives empirically at many shrewd and insightful perspectives on evil that are routinely ignored or denied.

5. Austin Farrer, **THE TRIPLE VICTORY** (1965). The devil's temptation of Jesus in the wilderness is our primary source for understanding the way the devil works, the nature of temptation itself, and how we can respond Christianly. As Farrer writes on this particular piece of revelation he does again what he characteristically does so well: he combines a disciplined spiritual imagination with astute exegetical skills and serves forth seasoned and mature wisdom.

6. William Golding, **THE LORD OF THE FLIES** (1954). The cultural pseudo-myth that shapes the Western imagination is that we are all basically good people and innocent of evil; all that is wrong with us and the world is a result of ignorance that can be put right by education. How this myth is able to persist in the presence of so much evidence to the contrary is one of the wonders of the modern world. This novel is a major assault on the myth.

7. Paul Ricoeur, **THE SYMBOLISM OF EVIL** (1967). We need all the help we can get in perceiving the presence and workings of evil. Ricoeur, a language philosopher, assists us from an unexpected quarter by examining our use of language.

8. Hannah Arendt, **EICHMANN IN JERUSALEM** (1963). Rarely in human history have sin and evil reached such monstrous dimensions as in the Nazi attempt at Jewish genocide — they murdered six million Jews before they were stopped. Adolph Eichmann was the Nazi bureaucrat primarily responsible for carrying out the planned genocide. When Eichmann was tried before a court of law in Jerusalem, Hannah Arendt reported on the trial. To everyone's surprise, Eichmann turned out to be a rather colorless, ordinary, law-abiding citizen. Arendt entered the phrase "the banality of evil" into our vocabularies. Evil does its most effective work when it is least noticed.

9. Herman Melville, **THE CONFIDENCE-MAN: His Masquerade** (1949). An old spiritual warns, "The Devil is a liar and a conjurer too, and if you don't watch out he'll conjure you." The devil never appears as the devil. James tells us that he appears as an angel of light. Melville wasn't fooled by the appearances. This novel, strange and quirky as it is, gives us a feel for what we're up against as we deal with this devil who never comes out into the open.

10. Thomas Mann, **DOCTOR FAUSTUS** (1947). The medieval Faust legend has provided a rich source for reflection on the subtleties of evil present in the human life. Many novelists and playwrights have used it, but none better in our century than Thomas Mann. This is a major text on the dark side of spirituality.

11. William Faulkner, **THE HAMLET** (1940), **THE TOWN** (1957), and **THE MANSION** (1959). This trilogy of novels tells a detailed and convincing story of sin and evil as it rises from poverty to prominence. Faulkner is among our finest diagnosticians of what Kierkegaard once named "the sickness unto death."

12. Aldous Huxley, **GREY EMINENCE** (1941)and **THE DEVILS OF LOUDON** (1952). In this pair of novels, Huxley shows us the particular ways in which evil enters religious settings and spiritual aspirations to corrupt and destroy. Anyone who works in a religious setting or gives spiritual leadership to others needs frequent warnings. The warnings served by these novels are true and timely.

13. Charles Williams, **THE GREATER TRUMPS** (1950). The spirituality of evil is elusive, for it has no substance in itself. More often than not the best way to become aware of it is through story. Williams wrote seven novels that are not exactly *about* evil, but in which evil always plays a significant role — even as it does in our ordinary lives. This one is representative. He shows us what to notice, trains our imaginations in perception so that we can more accurately pray, "Deliver us from evil."

14. Reinhold Niebuhr, **THE NATURE AND DESTINY OF MAN** (1941-43). In dealing with sin, it is easy to slip into a fussy moralism; in dealing with evil, it is common to succumb to doomsday hysterics. Niebuhr is neither moralistic nor hysterical — he is *theological.* He coolly, relentlessly, thoroughly penetrates the nature and persistence of sin and evil in our God-created, Christ-redeemed lives, personally and corporately. In facing what's wrong in us and society, very often we forget that we are working in a God context. Niebuhr never forgets — he is a true theologian, keeping us, our sin, and evil, steadily in the presence of God.

XIX

History

M ost of the books listed so far have been by writers who are doing/being/thinking spirituality. They are writing the experience of attending to God, discovering and exploring the connections, integrating God's creation and covenant in their own daily lives. They do not always explicitly name God or Jesus in their writing — much of spirituality is implicit. Glory and Mystery are sometimes best apprehended obliquely. There is a shyness inherent in spirituality that does not welcome direct attention.

It is easy to get bewildered in this company — such a torrent of energy and insight pours in upon us when we open ourselves to the influence of our spiritual masters. So we need the help of classifiers and historians and mapmakers. The books in this section are written *about* spirituality: describing what others have done, setting people and movements in their cultural, historical, and theological environments, sorting out the different aspects of spirituality and naming them. I caution my friends not to major in this — one of the classic dangers of spirituality is draining off energy by talking/reading about it instead of living into it. A competent informational knowledge of what others have done can easily mask an inner avoidance of prayer.

1. Louis Bouyer, **A HISTORY OF CHRISTIAN SPIRITU-ALITY**, 3 volumes (1982). A magnificent appreciation of the vast and intricate inner life of the church these two thousand years. Because there is so much intensity in spirituality, it is difficult to avoid sectarianism; Bouyer manages to maintain catholicity in the truest and deepest sense.

2. Brian Holt, **THIRSTY FOR GOD: A Brief History of Christian Spirituality** (1993). This is the finest brief guide to the history of spirituality that I know of. Succinct and accurate.

3. Kenneth Kirk, **THE VISION OF GOD** (1931). This is Oxford scholarship at its meticulous best. Wonderfully detailed and ruminative. Kirk searches out the centers of vitality in experienced faith from pre-Christian pagans and Jews through Bossuet and Fénelon at the opening of the eighteenth century.

4. Kenneth Leech, **EXPERIENCING GOD: Theology as Spirituality** (1985). Those of us who have learned our theology primarily as an intellectual discipline in an academic setting have to recover the older way of doing theology — as spiritual discipline in a prayer setting. The intellectual aspects are no less rigorous, but they are organic to spirit, not an abstraction of mind.

5. John T. McNeill, **A HISTORY OF THE CURE OF SOULS** (1951). I have a special fondness for this book: reading it was a passageway out of a pastoral spirituality that was faddish and parochial into one that was multicultural and centuries deep in wisdom.

6. Rowan Williams, **CHRISTIAN SPIRITUALITY** (1979). This British scholar is absolutely brilliant in his exposition of the source persons and writings in our field. All the old materials are thought and prayed through with freshness. Insights cascade. The range is from the New Testament to John of the Cross and Martin Luther.

7. Evelyn Underhill, **MYSTICISM** (1948). An exceedingly dull book, but full of useful information. When writing out of her own experience, Underhill wrote some fine books. But this one, while giving no pleasure in the reading, is valuable in ways her other books are not.

8. William Inge, **CHRISTIAN MYSTICISM** (1899). Inge, who later became a bishop in the Church of England, is interested here mostly in the philosophical dimensions of mysticism.

9. Ronald Knox, **ENTHUSIASM** (1950). Spurious forms of spirituality bedevil our best intentions. Knox tackles one especially persistent deviation from sanity and holiness and holds it down long enough for us to take a look that is both critical and sympathetic.

10. Martin Thornton, **ENGLISH SPIRITUALITY** (1963). When I realize how thoroughly Thornton knows, appreciates, and appropriates his Anglican roots, and what richness and depth it gives to his practice, I begin longing for someone to do something equivalent for North American spirituality.

11. Wolfhart Pannenberg, **CHRISTIAN SPIRITUALITY** (1983). The focus here is narrow: very Protestant, very contemporary, very academic. (But academicians are also welcome here!) These perspectives provoke insights that need tending to.

12. Andrew Louth, **THE ORIGINS OF THE CHRISTIAN MYSTICAL TRADITION: From Plato to Denys** (1981). For the first five hundred years of Christianity, most of the formative writing by Christians on God and the soul used the vocabulary and thought forms deriving from and continuing in the tradition of Plato. In some ways this was good, for it was a language well suited to the world of spirit. But it also has been the source of much mischief, for it introduced attitudes and concepts that are quite at variance with the Christian gospel. If we are to read our ancestors both appreciatively and critically, we need a competent guide so that in pursuing a life of prayer in Christ we are not inadvertently led off "the Way, the Truth, and the Life" into some mystical blind alley. Louth is a good guide.

13. Gordon S. Wakefield, editor, **THE WESTMINSTER DICTIONARY OF CHRISTIAN SPIRITUALITY** (1983). The standard one-volume reference work in our field.

14. CHRISTIAN SPIRITUALITY, 3 volumes, edited by Bernard McGinn and John Meyendorff (1989). The entire range of Christian spirituality is covered admirably by scholars from every part of the church and from all over the world.

XX

E. H. Peterson

Reading, for me, eventually turns into writing. For thirty-five years I have been trying to write a Christian evangelical and biblical spirituality that assimilates the diverse richness of our traditions and then works them out in the context of the North American experience.

1. **LIKE DEW YOUR YOUTH** (Wm. B. Eerdmans, 1994). This was my first venture into spiritual direction. I found that the people in my parish most avid for answers and counsel were the parents of adolescents. They typically viewed their teenagers as problems to be solved, and me as their partner in the solution. I started meeting with them and asked them to look at their experience of being a parent as material for *their* spiritual maturity, and their children as gifts to them providing stimulus to their deepening growth. After several years of these meetings I wrote this book. (This was first published under the title *Growing Up in Christ* by John Knox Press in 1979, then as *Growing Up with Your Teenager* by Revell in 1988. The current edition has an additional chapter.)

2. FIVE SMOOTH STONES FOR PASTORAL WORK
(Wm. B. Eerdmans, 1992; first published in 1982 by John Knox
Publishing Company). In a world and church in which pastoral
work has been heavily psychologized and sociologized, I am trying
to reestablish our work in vigorous worship and biblical narratives.
I found five small books in the Hebrew Scriptures that were
pastorally connected with the great events of worship, and use
them to show five areas of pastoral work that develop organically
out of worship.

3. A LONG OBEDIENCE IN THE SAME DIRECTION
(InterVarsity Press, 1980). I use the Psalms of Ascent (120
through 134) as a manual for discipleship, trying to counter the
American lust for easy answers and quick solutions by submitting
to these old prayers that were used "on the road" as pilgrims
worked their way up through the hills to the great acts of worship
in Jerusalem.

4. TRAVELING LIGHT (Helmers & Howard, 1988; originally
published by InterVarsity Press, 1982). The theme is freedom. The
source is Paul's letter to the Galatians. The triggering incident was
my congregation of suburban Presbyterians who seemed to me mired
in their possessions and security systems. Christians living in the
"land of the free" ought to have, I thought, a good deal more
spontaneity about them. My pastoral intent was to graft some of the
classic wisdom of spirituality into this immediate American context.

5. RUN WITH THE HORSES (InterVarsity Press, 1983).
Spirituality deals, along with other matters, with excellence. In
this context excellence is an aspect of holiness, living in robust
sanity. To give expression to this I wrote a kind of midrash on
Jeremiah to provide a blood transfusion ("the life is in the blood")
to the anemic, minimalist religion that I find all around me.

6. WHERE YOUR TREASURE IS (Wm. B. Eerdmans, 1993; first published under the title *Earth and Altar* by InterVarsity Press, 1985). Distressed by extensive privatization of prayer, I wrote this book as counterattack: to show how political the life of prayer is, that it works at the center not only of individuals but of communities, and of communities previous to individuals. Eleven psalms provide the source material.

7. WORKING THE ANGLES (Wm. B. Eerdmans, 1987). The "angles" are prayer, Scripture, and spiritual direction, the typical locations in pastoral work where we attend to God. First overwhelmed and then considerably angered by the shopkeeper mentality of so many pastor colleagues, I felt the need to establish God-attentiveness and God-responsiveness in my own life and repudiate religious marketing entirely.

8. REVERSED THUNDER (Harper & Row, 1991). John's Revelation, alongside the Psalms, has been a lifelong interest for me, especially as it serves to bring all things into prayer and worship. It is above all, I think, a pastor's book — written by a pastor in the thick of parish life. I have a focused concern here in showing how the praying imagination is a means of grace.

9. THE CONTEMPLATIVE PASTOR (Wm. B. Eerdmans, 1993; first published by Word, 1989). My conviction is that the pastor must refuse to be shaped by the culture, whether secular or ecclesiastical, and insist on becoming a person of prayer in the community of worship. This is our assigned task; anything less or other is malpractice.

10. ANSWERING GOD (Harper San Francisco, 1989). For most of the church's life the Psalms have been the school (or gymnasium) of prayer — this is where we learn to mature in prayer. I try to recover this foundational and (until recently) common practice of Christians for our century. In one way or another I have been brooding and writing this book for thirty years.

11. UNDER THE UNPREDICTABLE PLANT (Wm. B. Eerdmans, 1992). Using the narrative structure of the book of Jonah, I explore the vocational spirituality of pastoral work, looking for the resources that will nurture holiness in a vocation that is under terrific pressures that if uncontested reduce it to a secularized professionalism.

12. STORIES OF THE CHRISTIAN YEAR, editor (Macmillan, 1992). Several of my friends joined me in writing these stories, wanting to rescue the calendar from captivity to the merchants. These are holy days we are living, not shopping days.

13. SUBVERSIVE SPIRITUALITY (Regent Bookstore, 1994). Christian spirituality is worked out for the most part in decidedly uncongenial surroundings and circumstances. This gathering of occasional essays, addresses, poems, and interviews represents some of my efforts at articulating and living Christianly in a world that is no friend of grace.

14. PRAYING WITH JESUS and **PRAYING WITH THE PSALMS** (1993), **PRAYING WITH MOSES** and **PRAYING WITH THE EARLY CHRISTIANS** (1994), **PRAYING WITH THE PROPHETS** and **PRAYING WITH ST. PAUL** (1995, Harper San Francisco). These six books of brief Scripture readings, meditations, and prayers are each structured in a sequence of 365 days. "Lectio Divina" in fresh form.

15. THE MESSAGE: The New Testament in Contemporary English (NavPress, 1993). The writers of what is now our New

Testament used the common language of marketplace and home. It was not culturally refined; it did not sound "religious." And its first readers/hearers did not need a commentary to get it. My purpose in doing this paraphrase was to recover that same sense of immediacy and earthiness in our reading of our Scriptures.

16. THE PSALMS: The Message (NavPress, 1994). This is my first entry in what I hope will eventually become the entire Old Testament in the common idiom of North Americans at the end of the twentieth century.

Index of Authors

Index of Books

Index of Books